Presented to

_____

On the occasion of

_____

From

_____

Date

_____

Member of the
Evangelical Christian
Publishers Association

GOD'S WORD FOR SURVIVING THE REAL WORLD

DEVOTIONS FOR A NEW GENERATION

Toni Sortor
and
Pamela McQuade

PUBLISHING, INC.
Uhrichsville, Ohio

INTRODUCTION

You've waited a long time for this.

You're on your own, making your way through a great big world full of opportunity, adventure, and challenge.

So what's in store for you now? A job, that's for sure. It may not be the best job in the world, or even close. It might not be what you've "always wanted to do." But you have to start somewhere and begin to build a resume that fills at least one sheet of paper.

How about a place of your own? It probably won't be a palace. In fact, it might be too small and in need of some repairs. But it will be yours, and soon you'll be making plans for moving into a bigger and better place.

This stage of life is exciting, but it may be a lot harder than you've ever imagined. For much of your life, you've lived by other people's rules, and even though they were sometimes confining, at least you had some guidelines to live by. Now you have to make your own decisions. Do you spend money faster than you can earn it, snapping up all the latest clothes and electronics? Or do you develop the self-esteem needed to live within your wages and maybe even save a little? Do you spend your free time partying, or do you invest it in volunteer work or classes that will help you get ahead in your career? Do you stop going to church because your parents aren't there to wake you up on Sunday morning, or do you get up and show up on time? The decisions just keep coming.

To make good decisions, you need good information. If you're thinking of buying a particular automobile, you talk to others who own that kind of car and read the reviews in consumer magazines. If you're making a life-changing decision or debating a point of morality, you turn to the one source of good information that will never steer you wrong: the Bible. As God's Word, it can be trusted completely.

This book, *God's Word for Surviving the Real World*, will point you to some key passages in the Bible—passages that deal with the issues you'll face as you're out on your own. These devotions will lead you on an inspirational journey to spiritual maturity in your relationship with Jesus Christ. If you have never accepted Jesus Christ as the Son of God—and the personal Savior of those who receive Him—take time to read a few Bible verses (John 3:3, John 3:16, Romans 6:23, Romans 10:9) before you start this book. More than anything else, this decision will give you the wisdom and confidence you need to face life's challenges.

This book isn't a replacement for your Bible. But perhaps it can help you through this crucial time and point you in the right direction as you make decisions and choices, both large and small. Get ready for the adventure of your life—and read on for *God's Word for Surviving the Real World*!

WHEN THE WALLET RUNS DRY

A poor man is shunned by all his relatives—
how much more do his friends avoid him!
Though he pursues them with pleading,
they are nowhere to be found.
PROVERBS 19:7

What a sad picture! This poor guy's relatives don't want him around because he's an embarrassment to the whole family. And now his friends won't even return his calls. He doesn't understand. Sure, he's broke—but how could everyone turn on him like this?

This guy has probably become a pain in the neck. He has asked too many relatives for loans he will never repay. He's mooched too many meals and movies from his friends. His constant cries for help have turned everyone off.

His poverty probably isn't his fault. Stuff like that just happens. But obviously his reaction to poverty has been too extreme and he has driven everyone away. He's forgotten that it's not the amount of money you have but your faith in God that's important. Some people can handle both poverty and wealth with grace; others spend all their time whining.

Father, money is scarce right now. I know things will get better for me later, but I'm a little scared. Help me survive this with good humor and hope so those I love will never want to hide from me.

LEARNING HOW TO BUDGET

On the first day of every week,
each one of you should set aside
a sum of money in keeping with his income,
saving it up.
1 CORINTHIANS 16:2

I n the old days, budgeting was simple. You bought a flat metal lock box with compartments. Then you physically divided up your salary, putting one-quarter of your monthly expenses in each compartment. Of course, some expenses didn't fit any category, and at least one compartment usually came up short at the end of the month. But the system gave you some self-control.

You can set up a system like this on a computer so your bank account doesn't leak like a sieve. The important part—and the least fun—is sitting down with a calculator to figure out exactly how much money has to go in each compartment each month. A budgeting book from the library can help. It's not a perfect system, but it will tell you how long it will be before you can lease that car.

Father, I need to get a handle on my money. I need to know where it's all going and what I'm doing wrong. Give me the patience to sit down and do this budgeting—and then give me the self-control I need to make it work.

THE PATH TO RESPECT

The fear of the Lord is
the beginning of wisdom:
a good understanding have all they
that do his commandments.
PSALM 111:10 KJV

We all need to feel we are respected. Unfortunately, respect is hard to earn when you're young. If you haven't been with a company for a few years, almost no one will bother to listen to your good ideas, let alone act on them. Some supervisors will even steal your ideas, taking the credit that rightfully belongs to you! What should you do?

Two paths lead to respect, and the one you choose determines your future—so choose carefully. The first path comes most naturally. You watch your back, strike before you're struck, and butter up the right people until you've clawed yourself to the top.

What's the second path? Follow the principles laid down by the Lord. This is not the easy way. It's not a shortcut, and at times it doesn't even seem to work. But it will soon give you self-respect—the first step on the path to success.

Father, help me choose wisely when I come to life's crossroads. Give me wisdom to choose the Lamb's path, not the tiger's. Help me be someone who is respected for the way I live, not for the damage I can do.

OFFICE CULTURE VS. OFFICE POLITICS

*Now no chastening for the present seemeth to be
joyous, but grievous: nevertheless afterward
it yieldeth the peaceable fruit of righteousness unto
them which are exercised thereby.*
HEBREWS 12:11 KJV

It's a good idea to understand the distinction between office culture and office politics. The two are often hard to separate. Suppose, for instance, every man in your building wears a tie and jacket, even if they take the jacket off when they get down to work. Every woman wears dress pants, or a skirt, with a jacket. If you're a man, you may be tempted to buy one tie and skip the jacket; if you're a woman, you may think you can get by with jeans and a blazer. Eventually, though, someone is going to comment on your clothes. No matter how brilliant you are, when you buck office culture, you are not showing proper respect. People will notice.

Office culture is not the same as office politics. Office culture is a form of discipline that dictates how things will get done. It's an organizing force that leads to productivity.

Before you decide to rebel, make sure what it is you're fighting—office politics or office culture.

Lord, teach me to choose my battles carefully. Give me insight into my job's culture.

TURNING DARKNESS INTO LIGHT

For thou art my lamp, O Lord:
and the Lord will lighten my darkness.
2 SAMUEL 22:29 KJV

The holidays are over. All that looms ahead is winter, going to work in the dark and coming home in the dark. Winter can be lonely and depressing.

It's time to make some new friends. Easier said than done, of course. The bar scene's not for you. But just because you are a Christian, you don't have to hide away from humanity. The light of your faith can't shine in the world if you never get out into it.

Start with baby steps. Get out of the apartment. Do something—anything—that will let you hear human voices and interact with others. Next step: Volunteer. Forget about yourself and really become engaged in something outside yourself. Third step: Invite someone over. Host a Bible study that needs a home. Your apartment's big enough, no matter how small it is.

Soon your phone will be ringing, your weekends full, and you'll see the buds of developing friendships. You and the Lord will have turned your darkness into light.

Lord, I have much to offer others and am willing to work at sharing what I have. Help me keep my mind off my own darkness and focused on brightening the lives of others.

A Time to Marry

But since there is so much immorality,
each man should have his own wife,
and each woman her own husband.

1 Corinthians 7:2

Sounds like what your mother's been saying ever since you graduated, doesn't it? Some of your friends are happily married, a lot are determined to stay single until their biological clock approaches midnight, others are in marriages that are coming apart at the seams. You have friends who never stop trying to fix you up and others who applaud your singleness. Who's right?

You are! If you're single, that's what's right for you right now. You'll get all kinds of advice from everyone who cares for you, but never allow yourself to be pressured, either way. Marriage is an event of the heart, not a calculated decision.

When it's time for you to marry, you'll know. Suddenly, you'll want to see this one face across the breakfast table every day of your life. Marriage will no longer seem a threat but a promise.

Father, I want to be loved, but I'm not sure I want to be married. Give me confidence in my own feelings and make whatever I decide right for me, in line with Your design for my life.

A GOOD EXAMPLE

Let no man despise thy youth;
but be thou an example of the believers,
in word, in conversation, in charity,
in spirit, in faith, in purity.
1 TIMOTHY 4:12 KJV

When someone's referred to as a "good example," most likely that person is middle-aged or older. We tend to look to those who are older than we are for inspiration, figuring they have more experience and wisdom. That is not necessarily true; there are plenty of old fools around.

Don't rule yourself out of the good example population because you're young. Being a good example has nothing to do with age and everything to do with how you live your life. You can be a good example in kindergarten, providing you don't run with scissors.

You don't have to be a Goody Two-shoes, but you should try to live your life with courage and fairness and faith. If you can do that long enough, you're on your way toward becoming a good example. A good reputation opens doors that might otherwise stay closed to you.

Lord, I'm not sure I want to be a good example. Maybe for now I'll just concentrate on doing the right thing day by day and see how it works out. Teach me how I should act.

LIVING BY THE WORD

How can a young man keep his way pure?
By living according to your word.
PSALM 119:9

Finding time to read is hard—but why not dig your copy of the Bible out and put it where you'll see it every day? It has everything you need in it. It has plenty of action and suspense, not to mention memorable characters. If you run into something you don't understand, you can flip the page and find a new subject. If you're dealing with a problem in your life, the answers to it are in the Bible. Plus it can be read in short spurts. You can read a whole psalm while the bread is toasting.

Most important, the Bible will teach you how to live according to God's wishes. You can't be a good person without knowing what a good person does. Invest in a concordance and you'll be able to find everything the Bible says about whatever subject interests you. Then you'll know what God wants you to do. Life *does* come with an instruction book.

Father, when I have a question about what I should do in a certain circumstance, remind me that all Your answers are there for me in Your Word.

BECOMING A RESPONSIBLE PERSON

But let every man prove his own work,
and then shall he have rejoicing in himself alone,
and not in another.
For every man shall bear his own burden.
GALATIANS 6:4–5 KJV

Once you graduate and go out into the world, peer pressure lessens, although you will always have some pressure from the groups to which you belong—work groups, church groups, social groups, and so on. At this point in life, though, you have more groups to choose from, and their demands are more moderate, so you have more freedom. You have the chance to "reinvent" yourself. A shy high school student can choose to speak out in a new group. A follower can become a leader, or a leader can decide to take a break.

Now is the time to become the person you've always thought you could be. Carefully choose the groups with whom you want to associate. Assume responsibility for your own actions and take pride in the way you live, "for each one should carry his own load."

Lord, now that I have the freedom to be whomever I want to be,
help me make wise choices. I want to live a life I can be proud of,
and I know You have something special in mind for me.

Wholehearted Service to God

Serve wholeheartedly, as if you were serving the Lord,
not men, because you know that the Lord will reward everyone
for whatever good he does, whether he is slave or free.
EPHESIANS 6:7–8

Young people are noted for their vitality and enthusiasm. God likes that attitude so much that He promises to reward those who show that kind of wholeheartedness in their work, doing it as if they were working for Him instead of for their bosses.

Unfortunately, age and experience seem to take the edge off our enthusiasm. Some jobs just don't reward it. At first, employers welcome enthusiasm, but then it begins to annoy them. Like too much sugar, enthusiasm can become—well, just *too much.*

How do you strike a good balance? Look at someone older than yourself, someone well respected and successful at work, and see how that person operates. You'll see she's thorough in her work, quiet, and humble; but when she speaks, people listen. They know in her own quiet way, she's working wholeheartedly.

She probably started off just like you, but she was able to rein herself in until she learned her job. If you, too, can learn to harness your energy productively, you'll be on your way to success.

Father, show me how to channel my enthusiasm into solid work that pleases both my employer and You.

Our Will vs. God's Will

There are many devices in a man's heart;
nevertheless the counsel of the Lord,
that shall stand.
PROVERBS 19:21 KJV

There's nothing wrong with making plans—but ultimately, all our plans depend upon the will of God, and sometimes His will and ours are not the same. He knows when our plans won't get us where we should be, so sometimes He puts a roadblock in front of our carefully thought-out path and nudges us in another direction—while we mutter and complain about the detour.

This doesn't mean we shouldn't plan at all and leave everything to God. That would be aimlessly wandering around without purpose. We have to be flexible in our planning, though, aware that several roads may lead us where we want to be. We may not be able to see far enough ahead to plan the route, but God can, and His plans for us will never fail.

Lord, be patient with all my plans and dreams, even the ones You know won't work out the way I think they will. You've given me this need to look ahead, so it must be a good thing. Now give me the faith to trust You when everything falls apart, knowing You will lead me onto the right path for my life.

PURITY IN AN IMPURE WORLD

Let us purify ourselves from everything
that contaminates body and spirit,
perfecting holiness out of reverence for God.
2 CORINTHIANS 7:1

Unless you plan to live the life of a hermit, this verse is going to give you problems. We live in a thoroughly contaminated world where it's difficult to be even a little holy, let alone perfectly holy.

Start with the most important fact, though: Your sins have *already* been forgiven. How do you thank someone for saving your life now and forever? By trying to be what He wants you to be. No, you are not going to do it perfectly. Yes, you will still sin. But you will steer clear of situations that God disapproves of. You will treat your body as the holy temple of God, who lives in you. You will treat others the way you want to be treated. It's a start, anyway, and this is one case where good intentions *do* count.

Father, I can never live my life in total holiness, but I can show my thankfulness and reverence for You in many ways. Help me live my life in a way that will reflect Your glory and mercy and my eternal love.

KEEP YOUR MONEY IN PERSPECTIVE

Let your conversation be without covetousness;
and be content with such things as ye have:
for he hath said, I will never leave thee,
nor forsake thee.
HEBREWS 13:5 KJV

Love of money is not handling well what you have, investing and providing for your future. It's not even buying some things for fun. All of these are perfectly valid uses of money. God wants you to prosper and enjoy your success.

But He wants you to keep money in perspective. Money is good, but other things are better. Wouldn't you give everything you have to pay the bill if your sister or brother needed a life-saving operation? If a disaster made you abandon your apartment, would you save your checkbook or your roommate?

Those are pretty extreme examples, but you get the point. An excessive love of money can put your soul in danger. It can shatter marriages, turn family members against one another, and turn you into someone you'd never choose for a friend. Think about it the next time you deposit your paycheck.

Lord, I know You will provide for me. Keep me from the love of money. I want to be someone of whom You can be proud.

An Example to the World

But among you there must not be
even a hint of sexual immorality,
or of any kind of impurity, or of greed,
because these are improper for
God's holy people.

EPHESIANS 5:3

Once you declare your Christianity, your life is under a microscope. If you slip, all your nice words are useless.

You can't shrug this problem off by saying it's not *you* people should follow, but Christ, who was without sin. You are the one who makes Christ visible to the world. If you intend to be an evangelist, you'd better have your own life in order.

Does this mean you can't witness to anyone because your own life is flawed? Of course not. It does mean you have to voluntarily acknowledge your own shortcomings, admitting you are a flawed mirror of God; your own sins come between others and the glory you're trying to reflect. When you admit that, people can see you as honest, a normal human being, then look beyond you and glimpse the possibility of their own salvation.

Father, I'm not worthy to be an example of You and Your way of life. Help me deal with my own sins in a way that will bring glory to You and salvation to other sinners like me.

CARING FOR YOUR PETS

A righteous man cares for
the needs of his animal.
PROVERBS 12:10

L iving on your own is lonely. Eventually, you may start thinking about a dog, especially if you grew up with one. How nice it would be to open the door and have a puppy run into your arms! He'd curl up beside you in bed, protect the apartment while you're gone, and shower you with love.

But can you care for the needs of a dog? What would you do with him when you're at work? Let him tear up the apartment in frustration? Keep him in a cage? Your needs are important, but what would the dog get out of such a relationship, besides hours of loneliness? And what happens when you move, which most young people do often? Can you find a new apartment where dogs are allowed?

Righteous people take responsibility for the well-being of every animal they bring into their lives. Before you adopt that puppy, be sure you are ready for a fifteen-year commitment.

Father, I know it's not fair to use others, even a pet, to enrich my own life at their expense. Help me see this before I bring home a pet I can't care for properly.

THE TRUE FRIENDS IN YOUR LIFE

There are "friends" who destroy each other,
but a real friend sticks closer than a brother.
PROVERBS 18:24 NLT

Companions are easier to find than friends. They can be a little wacky, a little wild, a little irresponsible—but you certainly wouldn't want to introduce them to your mother when she comes to visit.

Companions come and go rapidly. They wear out their welcome or decide you've worn out yours, and it's no big deal when you part ways, since no one has any emotional commitment. You've had a few good times, that's all.

Of course you can't depend on companions for anything. If they're in the mood, they might help you move—once. They may lend you a twenty—once. But when you really need them, they'll be busy.

Fortunately, a few companions become friends. They hang around longer than usual. You find you have several interests in common and begin to talk seriously about deeper, more personal things. If you're really in tune with each other, you invest in each other, although you'd never say something like that. You'll just be there.

We all need friends like this.

Father, help me be careful in my choice of companions and willing to be a good friend.

WHERE TO PLANT YOUR ROOTS

And he said, "Verily, I say unto you,
No prophet is accepted in his own country."
LUKE 4:24 KJV

Jesus knew what many young people have learned through experience: If you want to get ahead in life, you may have to leave your hometown.

Why does it seem easier to get ahead elsewhere? For one thing, everyone knows you too well in your hometown. Even if they remember good things about you, you are still a little boy or girl in their minds, not a competent mechanic or stock market broker.

But not everyone can or wants to leave home. They work diligently, invest their time and money in their hometowns, and grow in the eyes of their old neighbors until they become town elders themselves. It takes a while, but the rewards are great, because hometowners love those who do well right where they were planted.

Whether you stay or go is an extremely personal decision. No one knows what you want as well as you do. Ask the Lord to give you guidance, then follow your heart. Besides, this is not an unchangeable decision—you *can* go home again.

Father, You know what I value most in life. Help me sort out my priorities and do what's right for me.

PROMISES OF LOVE

Many a man claims to have unfailing love,
but a faithful man who can find?
PROVERBS 20:6

When you're intoxicatingly in love, you always promise more than you can deliver. Let's be clear on one point, though: This type of promise is not the same as the promises we make when we marry. Those are not to be broken, under any circumstances. We're talking about impossible promises, such as "I promise I won't even *look* at another man for as long as I live." "I want you by my side every day of my life," you say, forgetting to add "except during football season."

We go on making promises like this because no one is totally sane when they are in love. As human beings, our love will always be as imperfect as we are. But with God's help, we can be faithful to the promises that count.

Father, help the one I love be patient with me when I goof up—and help me stay true to the promises that can absolutely never be broken.

MONEY TALKS

Houses and wealth are inherited from parents,
but a prudent wife is from the Lord.
PROVERBS 19:14

B eing prudent doesn't mean being cheap. It does mean being careful and thrifty. Some people are brought up to be savers, though, while others are spenders. A saver who falls into sudden money will still be a saver. A spender who goes bust will still spend whatever he has.

A couple that is mismatched in their financial philosophy is headed for trouble. This isn't something we usually think about when we fall in love and contemplate marriage, but it should be. After dating someone for months, you should have some idea of how he or she handles money. You're not looking for a perfect match. A person who is a little too cheap might do well to marry one who spends a little more freely, and vice versa. What you need is a person more or less like you, different within tolerable limits. Then at least you will be on the same wavelength when you discuss money issues.

In the end, you and your spouse will decide what is prudent, given your circumstances, so be sure you agree about your priorities.

Lord, help me spend my money wisely, and give me a mate who
shares my thoughts on this subject so we don't fall into the trap of
arguing about money and its uses.

WORKING WITH THE GOVERNMENT

Let every soul be subject unto the higher powers.
For there is no power but of God:
the powers that be are ordained of God.
ROMANS 13:1 KJV

God knows we need rules and regulations in society, or all would be chaos. The problem comes when we confuse our rulers with the governing system itself. We hate paying taxes, but we can't abolish the Internal Revenue Service and watch the government default on its obligations. No one likes to get a speeding ticket, but what would the roads be like without speed limits and people to enforce them?

As someone once said, the United States has a peaceful revolution every four years. If you are upset about the acts of a government official, get out there and vote.

God doesn't go into detail about governing authorities. He wants us to obey the laws we have created, but other than that, He left it up to us to form our own government. We're all part of "the system," and we all must obey its regulations—or change them in a peaceful manner.

Father, I know we have a human government, so it will always have problems. Give me faith in what we have created over the years and the courage to work toward peacefully changing what I don't like.

A Good Neighbor

A man who lacks judgment
derides his neighbor,
but a man of understanding
holds his tongue.
Proverbs 11:12

In a very real way, you made your neighbors the way they are. Most neighbors start out as neutral. They're willing to give you a chance because a good neighborhood is profitable to them, both emotionally and financially. If you go out of your way to be pleasant, so will they. If you're inconsiderate and rude, that's exactly what you'll get back.

So you're out on your own now, free for the first time to live as you please and play your music as loud as you want. You can party until dawn in your own apartment and let the garbage pile up as long as you want.

At first, the comments will be mild. "Good party, I heard." "Could you keep the music down a little?" "Did some animal die in there?" An apology and a slight mending of your ways can fix it all right away, but if you react with hostility, the police will be uninvited guests at your next party.

What exactly do you want your neighbor to be like? It's really up to you.

Father, teach me the rules of being a good neighbor. Remind me my neighbors have rights, too.

BETTER THAN A STORYBOOK ROMANCE

And Jacob loved Rachel; and said,
I will serve thee seven years for Rachel
thy younger daughter.
GENESIS 29:18 KJV

Such a storybook romance! Jacob loved Rachel so much that even seven years of service weren't too much. How could a woman resist such a man?

When you start dating seriously and things look good, stars light up your eyes. Your date seems perfect, and almost nothing would keep you apart. Bad weather and inconvenient schedules can't separate you.

But time has a way of changing that glow. Seven weeks (or seven months) later, when you know your date's faults better, you may wonder how Jacob held out so long. With your dating partner, you decide, he never would have made it!

Relationships weren't made to be worn like favorite T-shirts that are thrown away when they get ratty. Instead of picking on each other, prayerfully sit down and try to iron out your troubles. After all, Jacob and Rachel didn't have a trouble-free life, but they shared lifelong love.

Lord, I don't want to toss away relationships like old clothes. If I need to, help me work them out.

Pass It On

*I felt I had to write and urge you to
contend for the faith that was once for
all entrusted to the saints.*

JUDE 3

Feel as if no one ever trusts you?

God does.

Not only did He bring you to faith in Him, He entrusted you with the important task of passing it on to others, too.

If Christians never shared the faith, where would the Good News be? Should all Christians stop witnessing, destroy their Bibles, and disobediently ignore the trust God has given them, in a short time the world would be even worse than it is today. How many people would know what God has said?

During the early Middle Ages, Irish monks on the island of Iona carefully copied the Scriptures. While continental Europe was torn by political unrest and few people could pass on the Word, they painstakingly copied it letter by letter, keeping it alive. Because of their faithful efforts, we have the testimony of God's Word today.

Who needs to see or hear the gospel your life can pass on today?

Lord, I want to share Your Good News today. Show me someone who needs to hear it.

REKINDLE THE WARMTH

I am not writing you a new command but one we
have had from the beginning. I ask that we love
one another. And this is love: that we walk in
obedience to his commands.
2 JOHN 5–6

Sometimes being a Christian gets confusing. Pressures bear down, and your love grows cold. Spiritual winter sets in. So you start looking for something you've missed, some new trick to alter your life.

The truth is, you probably don't need a trick. You just need to get a handle on the old truth that's stared you in the face for a long time. Then you need to obey what you know.

When your love for God grows cold, take a fresh look at what He's already said. Draw close to the fire of His Word, and your life will alight.

When the cold, dull days of winter make you feel dull, too, renew your love for God. Warm yourself at the Scripture just as you'd seek the heat of a fireplace.

Jesus, I already know so much about You, but sometimes I don't use that knowledge in my life. Help me bridge the gap between my head and heart.

FINANCIAL PRIORITIES

"Will a man rob God? Yet you rob me.
"But you ask, 'How do we rob you?'
"In tithes and offerings. You are under a curse—
the whole nation of you—
because you are robbing me."
MALACHI 3:8–9

Billions of dollars are spent in America every year on R-rated movies. Each weekend, people throng to the latest violent blockbuster and plunk down their cash for entertainment.

Meanwhile, the view in other areas of America is hardly "entertaining." Churches can barely stay above water financially because so few people tithe, and some needy families only get help when their story reaches the six o'clock news.

Is it any surprise our nation is in trouble?

If we gave as generously to God as we do to our entertainment, imagine the people who could be helped. Churches could expand ministries to the inner city and support ministries all over the world. There'd be enough money to help a family get back on its feet following the breadwinner's illness.

God promises a curse to the nation that cheats Him, but the blessings that come with generous giving can hardly be imagined.

Let's start the blessing today.

Lord, entertainment isn't anything compared to You. Help me give to You first, not last.

WITHOUT GOD I AM NOTHING

Who am I, O Lord God?
and what is my house,
that thou hast brought me hitherto?
2 SAMUEL 7:18 KJV

Who prayed this incredibly humble prayer? Israel's greatest king, the man after God's own heart —David!

By the end of his life, David, who had received so much from God, knew better than to "obey" God on his own terms. God had told the king that his son, Solomon, would build the Temple; and even though David cherished this service for God, he humbly accepted God's decree.

After all, God had taken the shepherd boy and made him a king—he could also take the king and make him a shepherd again. David understood that without God, he was nothing.

When everything's going fine spiritually, you may want to do a great work for God and start planning it. Though you can't imagine why, suddenly it falls apart.

Do you go back where you should have started—prayer and obedience—or do you forge on, figuring it will all work out later?

Who do you think you are—a shepherd boy or a king?

Heavenly Father, when I want to serve You, I need to be humble.
Tune my heart to Yours, and let me never jump ahead of Your plans.

PHILOSOPHY AND VAIN DECEIT

Beware lest any man spoil you
through philosophy and vain deceit,
after the tradition of men, after the rudiments
of the world, and not after Christ.
COLOSSIANS 2:8 KJV

We expect the world to try to disagree with us. After all, those who don't know Jesus *aren't* going to believe everything we do.

But what happens when people in our churches face us with ideas that aren't biblical or philosophies that owe less to Christianity than something else?

It's nothing new. God hasn't forgotten His church. The Colossians had the same problem.

People in this New Testament church fought off heresy from within. No longer were the apostles' teachings and the Hebrew Scriptures enough. Among other things, the heretics taught the need for a secret knowledge and angel worship. They said you needed "something more" than Jesus.

If someone comes along teaching something "new" or different about Jesus, don't listen. God hasn't hidden anything you need to know about Jesus—it's all in His Book.

Anything else has no authority at all.

Jesus, I don't need anything "new" about You. I just need to know You better and better. Draw me close to You through Your Word.

GOD'S JUBILEE

For unto me the children of Israel are servants;
they are my servants whom I brought forth
out of the land of Egypt.
LEVITICUS 25:55 KJV

Freedom from slavery. Who'd give it up?
God had set His people free when they came out of Egypt
—they were only His servants, not an Egyptian's. But when
life became financially desperate, some Israelites sold themselves back into slavery to other Israelites. Perhaps the harvest
had been bad for years on end, and a farmer saw no other way
to pay his debts.

But even selling himself as a slave didn't mean he'd be
one for the rest of his life. Every fifty years, God called for
the Year of Jubilee. During this liberty celebration, Hebrew
slaves became free again. If he'd sold his land, he got that
back, too.

Even Israelite slaves were God's servants first and foremost. God had set them free, and no one could hold on to
them forever—that was His right.

If you know Jesus, God has liberated you, too. Nothing—
no sin or trouble or situation—can claim you forever.

You're free!

Jesus, thank You for making me free. I want to be Your servant first
and foremost.

THE REAL JOY BRINGER

Ho, every one that thirsteth, come ye
to the waters, and he that hath no money;
come ye, buy, and eat; yea, come, buy wine
and milk without money and without price.
Wherefore do ye spend money for that which
is not bread? and your labour
for that which satisfieth not?
ISAIAH 55:1–2 KJV

"Payday!" Jim shouted to his roommate. "Can't wait to get that CD player! I'll stop at the store on my way home—and oh, baby, will it blast tonight! Maybe I'd better pick up a couple of CDs, too."

Problem was, Jim didn't have the money to buy the equipment. He got into debt with the store, which charged him an exorbitant interest rate. Already the apartment stretched Jim's budget, but it didn't seem to matter. When he was short on cash, Jim just played the music louder.

One day Jim couldn't pay the rent, and his roommate got on his case. That night the CD player blared with a new album.

But a new CD player, new albums, and all the noise in the world couldn't make Jim happy. Things never solve problems, because they can't fill inner emptiness or bring lasting joy. The high from a buy only lasts a short time.

Invest instead in the joy bringer—Jesus.

Lord, You know the things I need. Don't let me become a spenda-holic when only You can satisfy.

GOD'S IMMEASURABLE MERCY

For God hath concluded them all in unbelief,
that he might have mercy upon all.
ROMANS 11:32 KJV

Are you *glad* that Adam sinned?
Well, in a strange way, maybe you *should* be, because if all humanity hadn't sinned, none of us would really know the Father's great mercy.

Our sin *is* awful. We shouldn't wish separation from God on anyone. Because of sin, we lead complex, messy lives.

Most of us would prefer not to get involved when a friend's own choices have landed her in nasty, ongoing problems — especially when those situations are likely to impact our lives, too. Could we blame God for wanting to ignore these difficulties we brought on ourselves?

But God, in His immeasurable mercy, didn't flinch from becoming involved in our grubby lives. Instead, even before we'd sinned, He'd designed a plan to straighten us out. Though it involved sending His only begotten Son, disrupting His existence, God didn't falter.

Seeing such mercy reaches deep down in our souls, changing them forever. Suddenly we, too, can get involved in higgledy-piggledy lives of hurting people, sharing the love that altered ours.

Lord God, what mercy You've shown me. How boundless the love
that brought me to Your eternal kingdom.

FROM REJECTION TO BLESSING

*"Blessed are ye, when men shall hate you,
and when they shall separate you from their
company, and shall reproach you, and cast
out your name as evil, for the Son of man's sake."*
LUKE 6:22 KJV

Sandy hurt when her best friend, Linda, wouldn't listen as she tried to tell her about Jesus. Sandy had just begun to experience a wonderful relationship with God and wanted to share it.

Being rejected was bad enough, but when she found out that Linda had started saying she was part of a cult, Sandy's heart ached. How could her best friend misunderstand her so?

In prayer, Sandy asked God, *How could this happen?* Then she opened her devotional, and the reading for the day was Luke 6:22.

Like Sandy, all of us have friends or family who misunderstand our faith. That doesn't mean there's anything wrong with us. We aren't necessarily saying the wrong words when we witness. From early in His ministry, Jesus warned us that people won't always accept our testimony.

But God can turn even rejection into a blessing.

Because of her friend's attitude, Sandy found some new friends—Christians—and one of them led Linda to Jesus.

Jesus, I want to share You with friends and family. Touch their hearts and open them to Your Word.

LISTEN TO THE SPIRIT'S CALL

"Whoever has my commands and obeys them,
he is the one who loves me."
JOHN 14:21

Betty Ann loved the Lord, but she had a hard time loving one coworker, Doris. No matter when Betty Ann took lunch, Doris was hanging around, waiting to complain about how terrible life was.

One day, despite her irritation, Betty Ann clearly felt the Spirit's pull to share her faith with Doris. Horrified, she did something she'd never done before—she refused to witness.

I just can't, Lord, she prayed. *My church has enough troubles without adding* her *to them. Imagine if she wanted to go to church with me!*

Betty Ann never did witness to Doris. Instead she went out to lunch every day to avoid her.

A week later, Doris got another job and left the company.

Betty Ann felt awful. She'd knowingly disobeyed God's command, and she could never forget that. Her failure burned into Betty Ann's soul. She confessed her sin and prayed someone else would have the courage to witness to Doris.

Disobedience always has a painful price. Don't ruin your love for Jesus by ignoring His voice.

Lord, keep me from disobedience and make my love for You grow each day.

"HERE AM I. SEND ME!"

Then I heard the voice of the Lord saying,
"Whom shall I send? And who will go for us?"
And I said, "Here am I. Send me!"
ISAIAH 6:8

Ever wish that you could rewrite that verse to say, "Here am I, send someone else"? When you feel overloaded spiritually, even though you'd like to comply, opening yourself to full obedience to God is hard.

Maybe, you worry, *if I give Him free rein, He'll send me to Timbuctoo* (or wherever your least-favorite place in the world is). *How could I ever cope with that?* you wonder.

If you're feeling overloaded, take your burden to God and confess that you've been hanging on to it. Then drop it in His hands and run! Don't stick around to pull it back out of the hands of the great burden lifter.

Then let Him lead you as you make decisions about ministries with which you're overinvolved, family problems that someone else needs to handle, or commitments you may not need to take on.

Pledge yourself to obedience, and walk in your new freedom. Don't let that old burden trap you again!

Send me, Lord, wherever You want me to go. I know You'll give me the strength I need.

BRICKS FROM GOD'S WORD

Every wise woman buildeth her house:
but the foolish plucketh it down with her hands.
PROVERBS 14:1 KJV

Wilma's marriage wasn't going at all well. She and Kevin never seemed to talk anymore, unless it was to quarrel. Wilma did talk to Kathy, though, who heard all her troubles.

One day, Wilma told Kathy about a guy at work. "I think he's interested in me, which is more than I can say for Kevin," she admitted.

Shocked, Kathy warned her against becoming involved. "Seek out counseling. I'm sure you can work it out with Kevin," she advised her friend. "If you give up too easily on your marriage, you may regret it for the rest of your life."

Some people seem to destroy their relationships with their own hands. They make unwise decisions, based on what they want today, without looking at the effects those choices will have on the future. A few years down the road, they're in trouble and wondering why.

The bricks and stones from God's Word give us the wisdom that builds a house no one can destroy—not even ourselves.

Savior, I want to build a strong, happy home, not one based on Satan's lies. As I study Your Word, show me the choices I need to make.

20/20 VISION

Jesus asked, "Do you see anything?"
He looked up and said, "I see people;
they look like trees walking around."
MARK 8:23–24

If you are nearsighted, you can relate to this man. Step outdoors without your glasses, and you may see trees as if they were covered by water.

Poor vision isn't hard to correct. You visit a doctor and get glasses or contact lenses. In a short while, you're 20/20.

But many of us with good eyesight don't recognize another kind of blindness—the moral kind. Even Christians can fall into this trap. Tempted by lust, we make excuses: *It's okay as long as I only go so far.* Or, *Well, we plan on getting married anyway.* We don't take a good look at the Good Book and ignore the clear commands written there. Fuzzy moral vision keeps us from knowing the truth.

Doubtful moral choices can make you feel uncomfortable deep in your heart. Peace seems elusive, and life is hard.

Feel that way? Maybe the soul doctor is trying to get your attention. Turn to the Great Physician to clear your vision.

O Great Physician, heal my moral sight. I want to see Your will 20/20 and walk in it every day.

"COME UNTO ME"

*"Come unto me, all ye that labour and are
heavy laden, and I will give you rest."*
MATTHEW 11:28 KJV

When you start on heavy labor—helping a friend move into his new place or digging in a garden—you work freely. It seems easy. But as you begin to tire, you set a goal: *I'll do this much, then take a rest.* Later, your muscles feel the strain, and thoughts of a break fill your mind. Finally, you just have to stop working. It's the same with emotional or spiritual work. You can't go on forever without Jesus' rest.

When you're working forty hours a week, hitting the mall after work, involved in ministry, and visiting friends on the weekend, by the time you get home, you're exhausted. Your Bible sits unused on your nightstand. Next morning, you scramble to the office, and a quiet time just doesn't seem to fit in.

Life's too hectic, you think.

Well of course it is! You missed the first part of this verse and didn't come to Jesus.

Lord, each day I need to come to You in prayer and through the Scriptures. When I'm feeling too busy, draw me with Your Spirit. I need to schedule a meeting with You.

A COPYCAT KING. . .OR GOD

*In those days there was no king in Israel: every
man did that which was right in his own eyes.*
JUDGES 21:25 KJV

That one sentence speaks volumes about Israel.

Over and over God had rescued His people. After moving into the Promised Land, Israel had seen Him defend them against the pagan nations. What more proof could they have wanted that their God was worthy of obedience? But by the end of the time of the judges, disorder ruled their souls—and their country.

When we resist God again and again, eventually rebellion burns deep into our souls. Though God has shown His mercy, we can no longer see it. We're abusing Him, so He finally gives us our just desserts.

That's what He did to Israel. Finally tired of their own misrule, Israel demanded a king, just like the other—pagan— nations. They wanted to become copycats of those who didn't love Him, so God gave them Saul—a copycat king who made them suffer in the same way pagan kings abused their people.

Don't put a Saul in charge of *your* life—give control to the Lord who rescued Israel instead.

*Jesus, I don't want to fall into a pattern of rebellion. Show me the
sins I tend to repeat and cleanse them from my life.*

DIFFICULT DECISIONS

"May you be richly rewarded by the Lord,
the God of Israel, under whose wings you
have come to take refuge."
RUTH 2:12

This blessing was given to Ruth, who trusted the God of Israel as she went with her mother-in-law to a land far from her home. Many people face a similar dilemma today. They move away to accept a job that isn't available in their hometown, leaving friends and family behind. In the meantime, their parents grow older, until eventually they can no longer live independently and their children face a hard decision. How should they care for their parents? Should they uproot themselves or their parents?

There is no "correct" answer. Every family is different, and no solution is perfect. This isn't a problem you have to deal with immediately, but you should think about it now and talk it over with your parents. You need to know what they want; they need to know what you feel willing and able to do when the time comes. You all need to know that God will spread His wings and protect you when you look to Him for help.

Father, thank You for Your help and protection. When I have to make these difficult decisions, give me the guidance I need.

TOTALLY COMMITTED

In everything that he undertook
in the service of God's temple and
in obedience to the law and the commands,
he sought his God and worked wholeheartedly.
And so he prospered.
2 CHRONICLES 31:21

King Hezekiah was totally committed to the service of God, seeking His will and working wholeheartedly. As a result, he prospered. Should we expect anything less if we commit our lives to God and wholeheartedly follow His will?

The Bible doesn't say that Hezekiah had an easy time of it. If you read his whole story, you'll see he worked harder than today's corporate leaders ever do. There must have been days when he was sick of all the organizing, rebuilding, defending, and other chores that fall on a king. He'd solve one problem only to have six others appear. Hezekiah wasn't perfect, either. He and the whole kingdom were punished for their pride when Hezekiah neglected to give God the glory for a miracle.

He must have been a wise man to rule successfully for twenty-nine years. But remember, Hezekiah was twenty-five when he became king!

Lord, teach me to seek Your will with all my heart and do it with the wisdom and enthusiasm of Hezekiah, the young king who was rewarded for his faithfulness.

THE FLIP SIDE OF WEALTH

The sleep of a labouring man is sweet,
whether he eats little or much:
but the abundance of the rich
will not suffer him to sleep.
ECCLESIASTES 5:12 KJV

Why can't a rich man sleep well? There's too much to worry about. A person without money to invest in the stock market never has to look at the financial pages. He can go straight to the sports pages without guilt. Someone who lives in an apartment never has to worry about the grass or the tree branch hanging over the roof. A dink in an old car is nothing to worry about; one in a BMW has to be fixed at great expense.

People with money usually end up buying themselves problems. Make no mistake, being rich is a lot of work and worry.

"We should all have it so bad," you may be thinking, but there's something to be said for a simple lifestyle. You can appreciate the sunset just as much in a rowboat as on a yacht.

Father, help me be content, whatever style of life my paycheck provides. I know You will see to my daily needs.

LOOK BEYOND THE SURFACE

"Stop judging by mere appearances,
and make a right judgment."
JOHN 7:24

O ur whole country is caught up in appearance today, almost to the point of making it an idol. We are consumed by the desire to be thin, to be beautiful, to dress with flair and style. All of these may be perfectly legitimate personal goals, but we can all too easily pervert them, try to impose them on others, and then judge everyone as unworthy who doesn't measure up.

Today the fit mock those who puff their way up the stairs. The beautiful recommend nose jobs. The tall look down on the small; those who look as if they need a good sandwich feel superior to those who have obviously had too many.

Jesus tells us to look beyond the surface, to judge actions, not appearances. We have no right to make our personal preferences the basis for judging the worthiness of others.

Father, just as I don't want to be judged by my acceptance of some popular trend, neither do I want to judge others by my own personal preferences. Keep me sensitive to the feelings of others and help me see the true person beyond the surface.

VIGILANCE FOR FREEDOM

For, brethren, ye have been called unto liberty;
only use not liberty for an occasion to the flesh.
GALATIANS 5:13 KJV

Political scientists say that constant vigilance is the price of liberty. Someone born free must take an active part in maintaining freedom, or rights will slowly be eroded away and freedom will fail.

The same is true in our personal lives. We are largely free to do what we please, within limits. Some of these limits are enforced by laws we've all supported since the Ten Commandments were handed down. Other limits are manmade for the good of society and are more open to quibbling. But, in general, we're pretty free.

This freedom requires constant vigilance. We are responsible for our personal lives. We have to watch our standards, obey the laws God made for our conduct, and recognize sin when we see it. Our God-given freedom must be protected, not abused.

Lord, help me use my personal freedom wisely and take responsibility for all my actions.

REWARDS OF THE RIGHTEOUS

To the man who pleases him,
God gives wisdom, knowledge and happiness,
but to the sinner he gives the task of
gathering and storing up wealth to
hand it over to the one who pleases God.
ECCLESIASTES 2:26

Wisdom, knowledge, and happiness are the rewards of those who please God. These rewards come directly from God, with no one in between. What goes around comes around, and the sinner ends up with nothing.

Sometimes life doesn't seem to work this way, but a lot goes on that we don't see, and we have to take the Lord's word for it, because this is a long-term promise.

More important, this verse helps us set our priorities. Our most important task is pleasing God with the way we live. If we do this, the rewards will follow. God Himself will provide us with the wisdom, knowledge, and happiness we need, and financial rewards will follow from them.

Sin, on the other hand, has no long-term rewards at all.

Father, I want to please You with my life. If my actions result in rewards, I will be thankful for them, but living my life according to Your wishes is the greatest reward of all.

THE HOPE OF A CHRISTIAN

*Unto the pure all things are pure: but unto them
that are defiled and unbelieving is nothing pure;
but even their mind and conscience is defiled.*

TITUS 1:15 KJV

A Christian looks at life with a lot more hope than a non-Christian. Sure, the world is full of sin, but a Christian should be willing to give everyone the benefit of a doubt. We slip, too, and it's not our job to judge others. In general, a Christian wants to see the good in everything and everyone.

Those without faith see the world as a dark, dangerous place where might makes right. Since they see everything as wicked, why should they be good? In fact, they soon come to believe there is no difference at all between good and bad—their consciences become corrupted.

It's pretty obvious which world view is most common today. Do you have the courage to think like a Christian? You'll be in the minority. You'll be called a fool, or at least naive. But you'll be happy.

Father, I don't want to see the world through the eyes of the unfaithful. Your world is good. You put it here for us to enjoy. Give me the courage to love Your world and everything in it.

NEED VS. GREED

"Take heed, and beware of covetousness:
for a man's life consisteth not in the
abundance of the things which he possesseth."
LUKE 12:15 KJV

Abundance of possessions isn't a big problem for a young person starting off. Lack of possessions is much more likely to be the problem. A person isn't being greedy when he wants a car to get to work or a new suit for a job interview, but if the car has to be a Mercedes and the suit Italian made, that's edging into greediness.

In the same way, wanting to succeed is not greed. Ambition is God's way of prodding us into action. But devoting yourself to success day and night, forsaking everything else in the climb to the top—well, that's greed.

As Jesus said, there are all kinds of greed to watch out for. Sometimes it's hard to tell when you've gone over the line. The next time you think you may be falling into greediness, give yourself the "tombstone test." How do you want to be remembered?

Father, help me distinguish between ambition and greed. Show me the right choices in how to use my talents and blessings.

THE FREEDOM WE HAVE

"Does the hawk take flight by your wisdom
and spread his wings toward the south?
Does the eagle soar at your command
and build his nest on high?"
JOB 39:26–27

There's a lot in our lives we can control and an awful lot we can't. Bosses and duties and family obligations hem us in, and sometimes we just want to shake them all off our backs and take control of ourselves again. Some Mondays we want to sleep until noon. Fat chance. Sleeping in on Mondays gets you fired, and being totally free is an impossible dream.

Even wild animals have laws they obey. How do birds know when it's time to migrate? Who shows an eagle the only safe place for her nest? Scientists have partial answers, but eventually they have to admit there's a lot they don't know about nature's laws.

If you've ever seen a salmon struggling against the current, scraping its skin against rocks and dodging bears that are hungry after a long winter fast, you'll have some appreciation of the freedom you *do* have.

Father, thank You for the choices I have in life. The next time I want to chuck it all, remind me my life is a lot better than most.

LET GOD BE GOD

" 'I will send down showers in season. . . .
The trees of the field will yield their fruit
and the ground will yield its crops.' "
EZEKIEL 34:26–27

Fortunately, we're not responsible for everything. Can you just imagine some international commission being responsible for the world's rain? They'd try to be fair. They'd knock down mountains that collect rain on one side and block it from the other. They'd seed clouds over parched land and discover twenty years later that the seeding caused cancer. They'd even sponsor worldwide rain dances.

But they would fail. There would be wars when drought struck and revolutions when floods arrived because *someone* would have to be punished for their failure. If you read any science fiction at all, you know that terraforming on a large scale brings more problems than it solves.

Better to leave some things to God, who knows what He's doing, even if we don't understand the whole process. We humans are a very adaptable species, and He is able to provide what we need.

Father, keep us from trying to control what only You understand.
Our sciences bring us wonderful advances, but our world needs to
be controlled by Your laws, not ours.

IN THE DUMPS

The Lord is nigh unto them that are of a broken heart;
and saveth such as be of a contrite spirit.
PSALM 34:18 KJV

You don't hear people talking about broken hearts these days, unless you are fond of country music, but they still happen to everyone at least once. You get dumped by someone you were seriously considering taking home to meet the folks. How could you have misread all the signals? How could something that seemed so good turn out to be a nightmare? What did you do?

Most of us turn into hermits for a while, dissecting the failed relationship over and over, trying to figure out what happened. Fortunately, friends put an end to that pretty soon, the unromantic fools. They drag you out of the apartment—or sit in it with you until you go out in self-defense. They tell you to get on with your life, and they fix you up. They nag you back into emotional health.

At the same time, God's doing a little work on you, too. Unlike your friends, He doesn't nag or fix you up. He's just there for you when you need Him, and He always understands.

Father, thank You for comforting me when I go and get my heart broken. I know if it happens again, You'll be there for me again.

TEMPTATION

*There hath no temptation taken you
but such as is common to man:
but God is faithful,
who will not suffer you to be tempted above that ye are able;
but will with the temptation also make a way to escape,
that ye may be able to bear it.*

1 CORINTHIANS 10:13 KJV

Temptations come in all sizes and shapes, from the seven deadly sins to sneaking a second dessert when you're home alone. As the verse above says, temptation is common, and God has seen them all. Even Jesus was tempted. It's not the temptation that makes you a sinner—you have to give in to the temptation to earn that label—and God is still in control of how much temptation comes your way. Better yet, as you begin to waver, He can show you how to get out of the situation. So the next time you are tempted to do something you don't want to do (or something you *do* want to do), thank God for His help and look for the solution He has provided for you.

Father, thank You for Your care whenever I'm tempted. I know I will never be tempted beyond what I can bear. You will give me the strength to resist.

AFFLICTIONS OF A BELIEVER

I believed; therefore I said,
"I am greatly afflicted."
PSALM 116:10

There's no question that being a believer brings afflictions of various types—minor martyrdoms. In some countries, believers are still being murdered. In ours, the afflictions are more social than physical, but that doesn't make them any easier to bear.

Some believers feel called to witness to their faith through words, wearing their faith on their shirtsleeves. Even doing this gently can lead to social problems. Others prefer to act as examples, witnessing through their acts and deeds. In some places, this is acceptable; in others, it's not. Every time believers say something or show devotion, they're open to minor martyrdom.

But you have to do what you have to do. Affliction is not the worst thing in the world. You can be afflicted by a disease —even the common cold. You can be afflicted by ambition, poverty, war, or even a tyrant of a boss. Since afflictions will come to you anyway, why not suffer the afflictions of a believer and do some good along the way?

Father, give me courage in the face of all my afflictions. I know You will care for me in any situation, and I want to do Your work.

INSTANT REWARDS

"Restrain your voice from weeping
and your eyes from tears,
for your work will be rewarded,"
declares the Lord.
JEREMIAH 31:16

Jeremiah always said exactly what he was told to say. He wasn't noted for being diplomatic or worrying about what others would think of his blunt words. In this case, he was saying, "Stop whining and get back to work. You'll get your reward eventually."

But eventually doesn't pay this month's rent, and we get impatient waiting for our rewards. We can have instant hamburgers, instant communication, instant friends. Why not instant rewards?

Jeremiah understood a lot about work, too. Nobody likes a crybaby employee who constantly complains about his work and its unfulfilling poverty wage. Those who go about their work cheerfully are much more likely to make a good impression and reap some rewards. Which type of worker would you prefer if you were the boss? Which type are you?

Father, help me be a cheerful worker who can patiently wait for my reward. Keep me pleasant to be near, not a complainer.

From Work to Reward

They shall not build, and another inhabit;
they shall not plant, and another eat:
for as the days of a tree are
the days of my people,
and mine elect shall long enjoy
the work of their hands.

ISAIAH 65:22 KJV

It's so frustrating to work hard and build something you'll never be able to enjoy. Maybe you spend your days tuning up cars you can't afford to own or roof houses that you will never be able to afford. It's not fair.

God promises it won't always be that way. His people will live long, happy lives and enjoy the benefits of their own work. Notice that the Bible doesn't say God will *give* His people everything they want. It says they will earn what they get.

The apostles worked to support themselves while they preached. Paul was a tentmaker by profession. As he traveled the world, he must have spent many nights inside tents he had made himself. A number of the apostles were fishermen who fed themselves through their own work on the Sea of Galilee. In order to enjoy the works of your hand, first you have to do the work.

Father, thank You for caring for my needs every day. I promise to do my part, too.

THE PROMOTION PATHS

Seest thou a man diligent in his business?
he shall stand before kings;
he shall not stand before mean men.
PROVERBS 22:29 KJV

Maybe you're thinking you don't care who you report to as long as the check comes every week, but experience will change your mind. Who you report to does make a difference. A change in your supervisor often means a promotion, a chance to have your opinions heard by someone with the power to put plans in action. It can mean the assignment of real responsibility.

You can get there by at least two paths: office politics or good work. Often the political route seems to work the fastest, especially at the lower levels. Some people rise like balloons until they hit the peak of their ability and explode. They can't handle the work.

The safest way to succeed is to rise slowly but surely on the basis of what you can do. You go up a level, learn the job at hand, and prove you can do more. Then it's safe to reach for another rung on the ladder.

Father, help me learn one job at a time and build my future on what I can do, not my ability to "look good."

A PURE LIFE

God wants you to be holy,
so you should keep clear of all sexual sin.
Then each of you will control your body
and live in holiness and honor—
not in lustful passion as the pagans do,
in their ignorance of God and his ways.
1 THESSALONIANS 4:3–5 NLT

Avoiding sexual immorality does not come naturally—it has to be *learned*—and there are very few teachers you can count on today. Society at large is pretty useless, issuing plenty of warnings about disease but little positive, practical advice for those struggling to lead a sanctified life.

So who is available to teach these lessons? The best teacher is God Himself, who can teach you what He expects through the Bible. Use a good concordance to look up verses about sex, love, marriage, and so forth. You can't obey laws you don't know exist, but all the laws are there in the Bible. Besides knowledge, God can give you the strength you will need to control your own body and live a pure life. Ask for His help when you need it.

Father, thank You for guiding me in all things. Forgive me when I disappoint You, and give me the strength I need to please You.

WHAT DOES THE LORD
REQUIRE OF YOU?

And what does the LORD require of you?
To act justly and to love mercy
and to walk humbly with your God.
MICAH 6:8

What does God expect of His people? That's Micah's question. Should they bring Him burned offerings, thousands of rams, rivers of oil? Should they offer their first-born children as payment for their sins? What will please the God who has saved them? How can they possibly repay such a debt?

The answer is to act justly, love mercy, and walk humbly with God. Whew! Is that it? What a relief!

Well, yes, it does sound pretty easy. But when you get down to specifics, it involves a total life change. In an unjust world, we are to be just. In a day when might makes right, we are to love mercy. In a life where we need to be our own public-relations person to get ahead, we are required to be humble. And while others follow the lead of movie stars, we are to walk with God.

Father, thank You for all You have done for me. I know I can never repay You with any offering less than my whole life. Help me to be just, merciful, and humble in my daily walk with You.

Sin No More

I am on the verge of collapse,
facing constant pain.
But I confess my sins;
I am deeply sorry for what I have done.
PSALM 38:17–18 NLT

Jesus was the only perfect person in the world. David, who wrote the verses above, was as sinful as the next man, yet God favored him over all other kings and chose his descendants to be the earthly ancestors of Jesus.

God knows we will sin. It's in our nature to do so. Not that we can use that as an excuse, but it is a fact of life we have to live with. God meant us to live happy lives, not be weighed down by an unnatural burden of sin. Jesus has accepted that burden for us. Give it over to Him, accept His sacrifice with joy, go on with your life, and try to sin no more.

Father, thank You for forgiving all my sins through Your Son, Jesus Christ. Let me dwell on what You have done for me, not on the many ways I have failed You.

THE STRENGTH TO STAND

And as they sat and did eat, Jesus said,
"Verily I say unto you,
One of you which eateth with me
shall betray me."
And they began to be sorrowful,
and to say unto him one by one,
Is it I? and another said, Is it I?
MARK 14:18–19 KJV

J ust the kind of firm believers you'd like to have following you if you were about to face the cross, right? Twelve men who aren't even sure of their own hearts!

Told that one would betray Jesus, for a single honest moment, not one disciple—not even brash Peter—guaranteed *he* would never give in.

But Jesus used these less-than-confident men precisely because they recognized their own weakness. God doesn't look for self-sufficient disciples who never err. He looks for those who know they are weak and know whom to turn to—Jesus.

If you're facing trouble and feel you lack strength to stand firm, don't waste your time worrying; turn to Jesus instead. You're in exactly the right place.

Lord Jesus, I'm so weak that sometimes I don't even realize it. When I face a cross, I can trust only in You.

THE "MESSIAH PICTURE"

Again the high priest asked him,
and said unto him, Art thou the Christ,
the Son of the Blessed?
MARK 14:61 KJV

Even the high priest was confused by Jesus. How could *this* man be Messiah?

Maybe Caiaphas expected a military leader like Judah Maccabeus. During the second century B.C., Judah and his brothers had briefly freed most of Jerusalem from Syrian rule. A Messiah who could *keep* Jerusalem free would have been to the high priest's liking. A military man who wouldn't make the high priest give up his power would have perfectly suited Caiaphas's expectations.

Jesus just didn't fit the high priest's "Messiah picture." Even after three years of His ministry, Caiaphas had a hard time believing He was right for the "job."

What is your "Messiah picture"? Do you want One who fights battles in your life—but won't expect you to give up control of it? If so, like Caiaphas, you probably have a different picture from the one in Scripture.

Get a perfect picture today—His name is Jesus, and He wants to be Lord of your whole life.

Jesus, I don't want to share Caiaphas's picture of You. Be King of my heart and rule my whole life.

EASTER'S PROMISE

And how the chief priests and our rulers
delivered him to be condemned to death,
and have crucified him.
But we trusted that it had been he which
should have redeemed Israel.
LUKE 24:20–21 KJV

A few years ago, in New York, the disciples of an elderly Jewish rabbi began proclaiming he was Messiah. Not long after, the rabbi died. Hope ended shortly after that rabbi's life. After all, how could an eternal God have a dead Messiah?

Two disciples on their way to Emmaus felt the same pain. Cleopas and his friend thought their faith in the Messiah had ended with the crucifixion. Hopelessness slowed their steps and sorrow filled their voices as they told the news to a chance-met "stranger."

This "stranger" showed them the truths of Scripture, and the disciples recognized Jesus. Hopelessness evaporated. They rushed back to Jerusalem to spread the Good News of the resurrection.

Does hopelessness blind you to Jesus' power in your life? Even when Easter is past on the calendar, it hasn't ended. Its promise lasts eternally for those who believe in Him.

Lord Jesus, keep the truth of Easter's promise in my heart the whole year. I need Your resurrecting power daily.

FLIRTING WITH SIN

" 'Return to me,' declares the Lord Almighty,
'and I will return to you.' "
ZECHARIAH 1:3

O nce he went out on his own, Jared didn't seem to click with the local Christian young adults. So he made friends with some fellows he met at work.

At first they seemed like good guys. Al always said good things about his family, and Don was a hard worker. But one weekend, they asked Jared to a drinking party. At first he said no. But after a couple of lonely weekends, Jared went along "just for the ride." Al got drunk, and Jared felt disgusted. But a couple of weekends later, all three friends were back at a similar party.

When he went home for Christmas and got tied up again with his church group, Jared realized the danger he'd put himself in. *What am I doing?* he asked himself. *I don't like drinking anyway.* He decided to look for some new, Christian friends, and he felt the Spirit warm his heart.

If, like Jared, you're flirting with sin, turn around today. Don't wait! The longer you stray, the harder it is to return to God.

Tempting as sin may be, help me resist it, Lord. I don't want to wake up one day and know I'm trapped.

THE GIFT OF GRACE

Some men came down from Judea to Antioch
and were teaching the brothers:
"Unless you are circumcised,
according to the custom taught by Moses,
you cannot be saved."
ACTS 15:1

People—even some well-meaning Christians—have a hard time accepting grace. They can't believe they don't have to add something to God's work. So they set up rules and regulations: "You have to do this, or you aren't a Christian." "You don't really love God unless you do that."

The men in this verse were trying to follow the Old Testament law as well as Jesus. They couldn't accept that His blood had done it all and that, when they accepted Him, their hearts, not their bodies, were circumcised. Many serious Gentile believers who wanted to obey God and feared setting a foot wrong did what these Judaizers said. Fear led them into sin.

God doesn't want you to be afraid, to worry if you've dotted all the *i*'s and crossed all the *t*'s that will let you enter heaven.

No, He loved you, so He gave you a free gift, no strings attached. Enjoy that gift today.

Thank You, Jesus, for Your grace. You've done everything that had to be done to bring me into heaven. I want to give my life as thanks.

OUR FAITHFUL GOD

Thou wast he that leddest out and broughtest in
Israel: and the LORD thy God said unto thee,
Thou shalt feed my people Israel,
and thou shalt be ruler over my people Israel.
1 CHRONICLES 11:2 KJV

David waited a long time to hear the Hebrew people remember this promise made by God. Jesse's son carried this assurance in his heart as he became King Saul's general, ran from the crazed ruler and hid in the hills, and battled Israel's enemies from afar. Though he must have been tempted to believe God had forgotten His promise, David still trusted.

The ex-shepherd boy, who had learned patience watching sheep, knew God would be faithful. But when life got stressful, he must have wondered *when*. David wished no ill on Saul, but he must have speculated on God's timing.

Sometimes, like David, we've waited a long time for a much-needed change—we know we need a raise in order to keep up with our rent—or we long for the end of a troublesome family problem. Like David, we don't know where the solution will come from, but we know it *is* coming. After all, isn't David's faithful God our God, too?

Lord, I know You haven't forgotten me. Maybe I just need to get on Your timing. Give me patience to wait for Your best.

TOOLS TO DEVELOP

*Therefore, among God's churches we boast
about your perseverance and faith in all the
persecutions and trials you are enduring.*
2 THESSALONIANS 1:4

Paul commended the Thessalonian Christians on their powerful faith, which had become the talk of the Christian world. The apostle boasted about them wherever he went.

Sure, you may be thinking. *I could be like that if I lived back then. It was easier for them.*

We'd like to think that. When our own witness seems weak, we assume others have it easier than we do. We excuse ourselves, *If only I had this. . . .* Or, *If only I were older. . . .* The *if onlys* could go on endlessly.

But the Thessalonians weren't armchair Christians. They suffered and endured trials. Many must have felt that being Christian wasn't always worth it.

Do we have to struggle so much? both we and the Thessalonians have wondered. *If only God would make our lives easier, couldn't we have a better witness?* we ask.

But trials and troubles are the tools God uses to develop His greatest saints.

Hold fast today!

Lord, some days the trials come raining down on me. No matter what my situation, let me be faithful to You.

SMOOTH TALKERS VS. ROUGH TALKERS

For there are many unruly
and vain talkers and deceivers.
TITUS 1:10 KJV

Some of the smoothest talking Christians are the least effective people spiritually. Though they have plenty of words and arguments and may look like they have spirituality all under control, their lives miss God's touch if they lack an obedient and truthful spirit.

Nowhere in Scripture does God command us to speak perfectly before we share our faith. Neither Moses nor Paul claimed to have public speaking down pat, but how they talked didn't matter. The Lord wasn't looking for con men; He used these leaders powerfully because they were obedient.

A smooth talker may deceive people. But even the most rough-spoken person can show people truth—especially the truth about Jesus. It's not in the words, but the heart.

What do your words show about your heart?

Whether I'm a professional speaker or someone who hates to talk, my words need to be honest and gentle to reflect You, Jesus.

LIFE ON THE EDGE OF FAITH

*"This poor widow has put more into
the treasury than all the others.
They all gave out of their wealth;
but she, out of her poverty, put in everything—
all she had to live on."*
MARK 12:43–44

Doesn't part of you wish you were as brave as the widow who dropped her last coins into the temple treasury? *How would I live if I gave that much?* you probably ask yourself. *What would I do?* Scary, isn't it?

Scripture doesn't tell us the widow went home to find money waiting for her. We can't guarantee that the story had that kind of happy ending.

But we know that, whatever happened, God knew what she had done and blessed her. Doesn't He promise to bless those who give?

Faith often means hanging on the edge, not knowing all the answers. Maybe for you it isn't putting your last pennies in the offering plate, but it's putting a tithe in when you don't know how you'll pay that last bill. Or maybe it's sharing the gospel with someone, when you don't know if he'll object.

That's life on the edge of faith.

Lord, I don't want to be so comfortable that I forget what life's like on the edge. Make my faith walk exciting.

HIS COMPASSIONS FAIL NOT

It is of the Lord's mercies that we are not
consumed, because his compassions fail not.
They are new every morning:
great is thy faithfulness.
LAMENTATIONS 3:22–23 KJV

Troubles seemed to overflow Craig. He spent more and more time on the job as his boss loaded him with work. His mom went into the hospital for tests. His girlfriend disappeared from his life. The pastor of his church resigned, and Craig wondered if *anything* in life was stable. Troubles seemed to eat Craig up inside.

Life's challenges can hit us hard—and suddenly. One moment you have one problem you're dealing with, and the next you have three or four. *Has God forgotten me? Will He leave me stranded?* you may wonder.

Never. Compassion is God's "middle name." *Every* day, even the lousy ones, He remains faithful. You may not see the way He's working, but He's out ahead, protecting you.

No trouble can eat you up when you belong to God. It may nibble at your edges, but you won't be consumed.

Lord, faith isn't just emotions. When I get that empty, stranded feeling, I know it's nothing You put in my heart. I don't want to be eaten up with worry—just consumed with Your Word.

THE LIGHT OF THE WORD

Thy word is a lamp unto my feet,
and a light unto my path.
I have sworn, and I will perform it,
that I will keep thy righteous judgments.
PSALM 119:105–106 KJV

Why should I read a book that's thousands of years old? What would those old guys know about modern life?"

If you haven't actually heard those words, you've heard that message from someone who doesn't value reading the Word.

The fact is, plenty of people, even those who've walked down a church aisle to commit themselves to Christ, have trouble spending time in the Bible. "I don't understand it," many complain.

But others pick up Scripture and new truths leap out at them, answering questions that have been on their hearts for a long time.

What's the difference?

Commitment. Spend regular time in the Word and seek out teaching on it, and the light goes on. Suddenly you begin to understand, and the Spirit comes alongside, teaching you new things.

At first you get out of the Word what you put into reading it. But as you get to know God better, that light burns brighter.

How's the light burning in your life?

Lord, when Your Word seems dry, keep me going. I want to draw closer to You.

ROAD RAGE

*"Whosoever is angry with his brother without
a cause shall be in danger of the judgment."*
MATTHEW 5:22 KJV

R oad rage starts as a minor incident—one car cuts off
another, and at least one temper flares. If you drive on
crowded roads, road rage may tempt you. You've had a rough
day at work, but the first time someone cuts you off, it's no big
thing. You remember you're God's child and hold back the
anger. Several miles later, at the highway entrance, cars crowd
you out. Finally you force your way into traffic, and a slow burn
starts. The next guy who cuts you off triggers that anger.

You'd never track down the offender and destroy him.
You just honk your horn or roll down the window and give
him a piece of your mind. What's wrong with that?

No physical roadkill occurred, just spiritual roadkill. God
doesn't tell us to get angry when we've had enough or when
the day's been miserable. He tells us *never* to give in to anger.

Why add God's judgment to an already bad day?

*Father, I want even my driving to reflect Your love. When I get
behind the wheel, cover me with Your peace.*

FROM TRIALS TO BLESSING

At the same time that my sanity was restored,
my honor and splendor were returned
to me for the glory of my kingdom. . . .
I was restored to my throne and
became even greater than before.
DANIEL 4:36

Nebuchadnezzar got so caught up in his own power as the king of Babylon that God humbled him. The king became like a wild animal. For seven years, he lost his sanity and became a wild man who ate grass.

At the end of those years, the proud ruler turned to God, and his sanity returned. Once Nebuchadnezzar recognized God's dominion, his kingdom was never the same. God restored all he had lost and much more—He made him even greater!

Like the king of Babylon, do you resist God, fearful that He'll overthrow your little kingdom and make you do everything you hate?

Then it's not Jesus you're thinking of.

God is a wonderful, generous Lord. Obey Him, and life's trials bring you better things, not destruction. He doesn't want to ruin your world, but to bless you beyond your expectations.

It's hard to believe You want me to have good things, Lord, when I focus on this world. Turn my eyes to You and give me a vision of Your blessing.

GOD HOLDS YOUR FUTURE

*I will cut off . . . them that worship the host
of heaven upon the housetops.*
ZEPHANIAH 1:4–5 KJV

B ut the occult is dangerous," Brendan warned his church
group. "Why—"

Another group member quickly cut him off, pooh-poohing his words. Some in the study didn't want to admit that reading a horoscope was unbiblical.

Knowing Christ isn't a cheap guarantee that you can do anything you like and still spend eternity in heavenly bliss. Dabbling in astrology, palm reading, and Tarot cards isn't something God ignores in His people.

Zephaniah took the people of Judah to task for a similar divided allegiance. He never said that they didn't give God a piece of their lives. They did—but they held on to Baal worship, too. They looked to the stars for answers, as well as going to the temple.

God doesn't save a piece of your life, He saves all of it. A faithful response is to give Him your whole life in return. You can't do that if you're also trying to use occult methods to see what the future holds.

You may not know your whole future, but you know who holds it. Trust in Him.

Thank You, Lord, for holding my future. I want to trust You for everything.

GOD WILL PROVIDE

"You have planted much, but have harvested little.
You eat, but never have enough.
You drink, but never have your fill.
You put on clothes, but are not warm.
You earn wages, only to put them
in a purse with holes in it."
HAGGAI 1:6

Sandy didn't have the best-paying job in the world, but she used her money carefully and could always pay her bills and give a tithe.

Her friend Alan rarely gave to the church, made twice as much money as Sandy, but never seemed to have a dollar in his pocket.

Some people reach the end of the month with their bills paid and their minds peaceful. Others always seem to need money, no matter how much they toss into their accounts.

You need to live below your income, spending less than you make. But no matter how much you make and how hard you try to keep a handle on it, if you don't give to God, there will be an empty hole in your pocket and a deeper one in your heart.

Obey Him, and somehow you'll have enough for all your needs.

Thank You, Father, for providing for all my needs. I want to give generously to You and do Your will today.

THE NAME OF JESUS

And the Lord shall be king over all the earth:
in that day shall there be one Lord,
and his name one.
ZECHARIAH 14:9 KJV

The name of Jesus used to grate against my nerves. Saying it was like squealing chalk against a blackboard," Alicia remembered. "I think, even before I knew Him, I couldn't get away from His authority."

There *is* something about the name of Jesus. Work in a factory, and you'll hear it uttered often, but not prayerfully. Yet who misuses the name of Allah, Buddha, or any other religious figure, when things aren't going right? It's as if even people who don't believe in Jesus can't get away from His authority. Maybe they blame Him for anything that goes wrong, but they unknowingly recognize Him.

One day Jesus will return to rule the entire earth. Then, at His name, "every knee should bow" (Philippians 2:10). Christians will kneel willingly, glorifying the Risen One, but nonbelievers will be forced to acknowledge their Judge.

Today recognize Jesus for who He is. There's a lot of power, glory, and love in that name.

Lord, Your name is wonderful. I want the world to know it today.

CARING FOR THE TEMPLE OF THE HOLY GHOST

What? Know ye not that your body is the temple
of the Holy Ghost which is in you,
which ye have of God?
1 CORINTHIANS 6:19 KJV

How long has it been since you've seen a dentist? Have you had your eyes checked once since leaving home? Had your blood pressure taken lately?

Probably not. Once we're responsible for our own bodies, we tend to ignore them until something goes wrong. A throbbing tooth will get us to a dentist pretty fast, but we'll skip the six-month checkups until then. Of course, a regular checkup would have caught the tiny cavity that's now big enough to drive a truck through.

In the old days, when you paid for health care out of your own pocket, you might have had economic reasons for avoiding medical costs, but now most people are covered by health insurance. Use it. Regular checkups will save you a lot of problems later. You won't be twenty-something forever. Don't you want a mouth full of your own teeth when you hit fifty?

Father, remind me to take care of myself now so I can enjoy good health later in life.

HEALTHY EATING

And having food and raiment
let us be therewith content.
1 TIMOTHY 6:8 KJV

What do you have for breakfast these days? A cup of coffee from 7-Eleven? Do you skip lunch and grab a candy bar? Is dinner a hamburger and fries?

Most people who leave home to live on their own change their eating habits. Who has time to make a meat loaf or pot roast? Who knows how? It's a great feeling to be able to eat whatever and whenever you want, with no one prodding you to eat your vegetables.

But your body does have certain requirements and will tell you when it needs a shot of something green. When it does, listen to it. Find a good salad bar if you're not up to washing lettuce. Take a daily vitamin pill to be sure you're filling in the blanks in your diet. Find a fast-food place that serves "comfort food"—the food you were brought up on. Don't neglect your body's nutritional needs for too long, or it will begin to punish you.

Father, I believe my body is Your temple, and I need to take care of it. Show me how I can eat properly in the small amount of time I have available.

THE NEED FOR CHURCH

We must pay more careful attention,
therefore, to what we have heard,
so that we do not drift away.
HEBREWS 2:1

All your life, Mom and Dad have taken responsibility for getting you to church, but that's over now. You may live miles from them or in the same town, but except for a little nagging, they can't control your actions anymore. It's on your head if you don't get yourself to church.

There are all kinds of excuses you can use, from not being able to find a friendly congregation to not feeling the need for church. It's easy to drift away, once your old habits have been broken and you're living in a new situation.

But Sunday's not the same without church. There's something nice missing from your week, even if you can't pinpoint it. Maybe Mom and Dad were right, and you need to pay more careful attention to what you have heard—from them and the Lord. Maybe it's time to find that friendly congregation and admit that you *need* to go to church.

Father, it's so easy to drift away from old habits, even the good ones. Help me remember the warmth of fellowship, the security of being part of a congregation, and my need for You.

REMEMBER YOUR CREATOR

Remember now thy Creator in the days
of thy youth, while the evil days come not,
nor the years draw nigh, when thou shalt say,
I have no pleasure in them.
ECCLESIASTES 12:1 KJV

Right now is one of the best times of your life. You are young and strong, unafraid of the future, and eager to experience all that life will bring. Now is the time to remember your Creator and thank Him for everything He has given you. Now is the time to enjoy yourself, sing His praises, and keep His commandments.

Remember how you used to thank your mom when she gave you your favorite food for dinner or took you on a great vacation? You thanked her with your whole heart and happily obeyed her rules. The days she gave you Brussels sprouts, you undoubtedly did not thank her—or take the garbage out without complaining. It works the same way in your relationship with God. Now, while things are going well, be lavish in your thanks, because it will be harder to do as life gets harder.

Father, thank You for the joys of life I see all around me today. Teach me now, while I am still young, how to live in a way that pleases You.

WHAT ABOUT MARTYRDOM?

And others had trial of cruel mockings and
scourgings, yea, moreover of bonds and
imprisonment: They were stoned, they
were sawn asunder, were tempted, were slain
with the sword: they wandered about
in sheepskins and goatskins;
being destitute, afflicted, tormented;
(Of whom the world was not worthy).
HEBREWS 11:36–38 KJV

Most of us will never have to face death for our faith, but there are dangers in feeling too safe. For one thing, someone in a safe country never even thinks about martyrdom —*personal* martyrdom. We aren't prepared for it and have no idea how we would react to that type of danger. What would you do if you had to renounce your faith in order to live? What would you do to keep your children alive? You can't make these decisions wisely and rationally when someone's pointing a gun at your head, and there won't be any chance to change your mind. Think about it now, while there's time —just in case.

Father, I don't even want to think about this happening to me, but give me the strength to do so and the courage to do what I have to do if the time should ever come.

WHAT HAPPENED TO RESPECT?

" 'Rise in the presence of the aged,
show respect for the elderly
and revere your God.' "
LEVITICUS 19:32

Parents have always taught basic manners: Cover your mouth when you cough, don't scratch in public, and so on, but lately manners have been ignored in our rush toward equality and self-expression. Life has become much less civil than it used to be.

We're not talking about how to tell a fish fork from a salad fork or the proper way to curtsey to royalty, neither of which has much to do with life today. We're talking about a general lack of respect for everyone, which leads to road rage, physical attacks on teachers, and other undesirable social acts.

Manners are not meaningless rules that only apply to the well-off. They are about well-earned respect and consideration for others. Think about the consequences of your action the next time you roll down your car window and prepare to show another driver what you think of him. Is this an act that is going to make the world a better place?

Father, my daily actions should be worthy of You. Help me show proper respect to all people, even when I'm upset and angry. Remind me of my manners and the great effect that even a simple thank-you can have on the world.

THE BEAUTY OF NATURE

*For, lo, the winter is past, the rain is over and
gone; The flowers appear on the earth;
the time of the singing of birds is come,
and the voice of the turtle is heard in our land.*
SONG OF SOLOMON 2:11–12 KJV

Even the hardest winter eventually gives way to spring, and signs of new life surround us. And yet nature has become irrelevant to many of us who live and work in a climate-controlled life. The closest most of us get to nature is when we're splashed by a taxi or the buses are thrown off schedule by snow and we're late for work. Nature is mostly a matter of inconvenience to us.

And yet nothing can make us feel as fully human as nature, if we get out there and really experience it. Spend some time out there and your whole outlook on life can change. Nature has no patience with self-involved humans. It humbles us, sometimes it hurts us, but it also teaches us that God is pleased with *all* His creations, and we are only one of them.

Lord, sometimes I forget about the breadth of Your creation and feel I am the only one who counts. Give me the opportunity to become more involved with all of Your creation so I can see myself in perspective.

STRANGERS IN THIS WORLD

*And if ye call on the Father, who without
respect of persons judgeth according to
every man's work, pass the time of
your sojourning here in fear.*
1 PETER 1:17 KJV

The world thinks in the present tense. Christians tend to think in the future tense, with a good understanding of the past. Like anyone else, they want to be successful, but they know God's will for their lives is more important. They are willing to give up a lot to lead righteous lives, knowing their rewards may be far in the future. They praise God for all His blessings in good times and in bad. Christians start with God and work down to themselves.

Anyone who thinks in such a totally different way is bound to be a stranger here, not quite at home in this world. A far better world awaits Christians, the place they can truly call home. Living as strangers is not easy, but it's the only way that makes any sense.

Lord, thank You for the salvation that is mine for the asking. If it causes me to feel like a stranger here, remind me that my home is with You.

JUST GOD/UNJUST WORLD

He is the Rock, his work is perfect:
for all his ways are judgment: a God of truth and
without iniquity, just and right is he.
DEUTERONOMY 32:4 KJV

For centuries wise men and women have had a hard time with this verse, so it's not unusual for the average person to ask the obvious question: If God is just, why isn't His world? Why don't the good prosper and the evil fail? Why do starvation and genocide still rage today?

One obvious answer is that God is working with flawed materials—us. Over the course of history, we've changed the world, not always for the better. He gave us dominion over the earth, and our sin has corrupted a perfectly just situation, which does not change the fact that God Himself is still what He has always been.

Maybe the best answer to the just-God/unjust-world problem is to admit that we don't know what's going on. We're simply not seeing the whole picture. Even if we could, we probably wouldn't understand it. Some things you just have to take on faith. God is still in the world, doing what only He can do.

Father, I place my life in Your hands, certain that all things work according to Your will, whether I understand or not.

CHILDREN OF LIGHT

Ye are all the children of light,
and the children of the day:
we are not of the night,
nor of darkness.

1 THESSALONIANS 5:5 KJV

There's nothing wrong with the night in itself. It's a time of peace and rest and relaxation, which we all need. A child of the light—a Christian—can enjoy both day and night.

Yet there is something about the night that worries us. Not many horror movies are filmed in bright daylight, and echoing footsteps behind us in the night can raise the hairs on the back of our neck. There's a sense of danger in the night that we can never completely escape. Maybe that's part of its attraction.

The trick is to be able to enjoy the night without taking it into our souls and becoming part of it. As Christians, we have seen the light and know wrong from right. We shouldn't do anything in the dark that we wouldn't do in the sunshine. We cannot *belong to* the night because we belong to Jesus.

Lord, You bring sunshine into my life where once there was darkness. Thank You for Your love and protection at all hours of the day and night.

ROAD MAPS

"Set up road signs; put up guideposts.
Take note of the highway,
the road that you take."
JEREMIAH 31:21

We all have to see the path we're walking, or we'll end up in the bushes, not where we thought we were going. Life's a pretty long road, so putting up a few mental road signs is a good idea. When you hit a crossroads, get out your ethical road map and choose your path deliberately. You'll either decide, "No, I don't want to go there," or, "Yes, this is the way."

Note that this is *your* road map; we each have to draw our own. You can give advice to other travelers you meet along the way, but you can't force them to follow your path. In the same way, you can't blindly follow some other traveler, hoping she's going where you want to go. If she suddenly veers off on a side road you don't know, you'll never find your way back to the right path. Be aware of your decisions and follow the way you know is right.

Father, there are so many choices I have to make in my life, and I can't see where they lead in the end. Give me Your guidance so I will end up next to You.

Can You Be Trusted with Much?

"Whoever can be trusted with very little
can also be trusted with much,
and whoever is dishonest with very little
will also be dishonest with much."

Luke 16:10

You're just starting off in your job, and nobody trusts you with very much. You do what you're told, day after day, and it gets pretty boring after a while. Where's the challenge? What do you have to do before you get to make a few decisions or enjoy some responsibility?

Unfortunately, you have to keep on doing just what you're doing now—only better. You have to master the boring stuff first, really get it down pat, and be the best "nobody" anyone's ever seen. Don't think no one's watching, because they are. Even boring work has to be done well, and if you sleepwalk through the day, it will be noticed. But if you prove yourself trustworthy in this job, a better one will be ahead for you. At the very least, you'll end up with a good reference for your resume.

Father, when my work gets so boring I want to nod off about mid-afternoon, remind me that I hold the keys to my own success in my own hands. I may be a nobody now, but I won't be for long, with Your help.

RIGHTEOUS ANGER

So have I sworn that I would not be wroth
with thee, nor rebuke thee.
ISAIAH 54:9 KJV

The last time God really lost His temper, He killed off everyone in the world except Noah and his family and a representative sample of every animal that filled the world. God must have known that humans can't live with a threat like that hanging over their heads, and He promised that sort of mass punishment was a thing of the past. Humanity itself was safe, even though individuals still had to deal with individual judgment. God promised to differentiate between individuals and humanity as a whole.

Besides taking a load of fear off our backs, this promise also serves as an example of how we should deal with our own anger. We have to differentiate, too. Just because a bald man fired you doesn't mean all bald men are to be hated. You can't hate all women when one breaks your heart. You don't kick all dogs after one bites your leg. If God, in His righteous anger, promises not to punish by category, can we do anything less?

Father, thank You for judging fairly, no matter how we displease You with our actions. Teach me to do the same.

CONTROL OVER ANGER

A quick-tempered man does foolish things.
PROVERBS 14:17

People handle anger in various ways. Some manage to push it down and continue as if they never felt it (probably giving themselves ulcers in the process). Others kick chairs in private but soon come to terms with their anger. Still others blow up and immediately feel better. We tend to react to anger the same way our parents did, for better or for worse.

In the same way, we all have different boiling points. It takes a lot to get some people angry, while others erupt at the slightest provocation.

However you react to anger, you need to maintain control. Anger makes us stupid. We do and say things we would never do under normal circumstances, starting fistfights or saying words we can never take back.

When anger takes over, we need to get away if we can't control ourselves. Go hide out in the rest room, if necessary. Shut a door behind you until you are back in control. A real man does not hit. A strong woman asserts control over herself, not over others.

Father, when I want to strike out in anger, whether verbally or physically, give me the self-control I need to avoid doing anything stupid.

GOOD ADVISORS

*Go from the presence of a foolish man, when
thou perceivest not in him the lips of knowledge.*
PROVERBS 14:7 KJV

A lot of foolish people are fun to be with. They tend to be
the life of the party, always a little wild and irresponsible, doing things we would never dream of doing and collecting followers like a magnet collects paper clips. Some of them are good people and loyal friends, too. They're a little stupid at times, but harmless.

Most of them, however, you wouldn't trust for good advice, for the serious decisions we all have to make. For that, we seek out someone a little more mature and probably a lot more boring, people who actually have a serious side. You can ask advice of the life of the party, but you have to take what he says with a grain of salt, never sure if he's being serious or just pulling your leg.

Father, help me choose my advisors carefully and not be pulled in by charm when what I need is a carefully thought-out response.

PROVE YOUR MATURITY GENTLY

Do not rebuke an older man harshly,
but exhort him as if he were your father.
1 TIMOTHY 5:1

That older guy makes you nuts! All you hear from him is the things you can't do, to the point where you wonder if you'll ever be old enough to walk a dog.

Some terrific people twenty, thirty, and even forty years older than you have positive outlooks and encourage you in most things you take on. They're joyful people, and you're glad to be around them.

But that one person. . .

When your personal naysayer starts carping, your mind lists all the ways you'd like to respond. *I'm not a baby anymore, I have a place of my own. You know, my boss trusts me more than you do.* Hold on—long enough to toss those words out of your mind. Exploding won't improve your situation. He'll just go away thinking he was right after all. Instead, prove your maturity by treating him gently.

Timothy was a young pastor trying to lead older folks. Some didn't want to listen, so Paul advised him to talk to the older generation, not blow up.

Take Paul's advice, and they'll eventually respect you.

When others doubt my maturity, Lord, help me curb my anger and answer with love.

SPIRITUAL JUNK FOOD

These men are blemishes at your love feasts,
eating with you without the slightest qualm—
shepherds who feed only themselves.

JUDE 12

Godless men had slipped into the church, misleading the brethren, seducing them to believe they could continue to sin and never receive God's correction. Jude called these false teachers "shepherds who only feed themselves."

Can you imagine a shepherd sitting on a barren hill, hungry animals all around him, enjoying his lunch? The baas and bleating would almost deafen him. He'd have to care for them.

Unlike sheep, people who fall in with wrong teaching rarely recognize the emptiness of what they're taking in. Instead, they keep following, filling their hearts with useless calories of spiritual junk food, never understanding that they're barely being fed at all.

Don't follow false teachers. They're here today, gone tomorrow. Nothing they do can last because they aren't founded on the bedrock of God's Word.

Lord, I don't want to be a wrong teacher any more than I want to follow one. Make my words reflect Your truth, and help my ears discern anything that doesn't reflect You.

GOD IS NO WIMP

God is jealous, and the Lord revengeth;
the Lord revengeth, and is furious;
the Lord will take vengeance on his adversaries,
and he reserveth wrath for his enemies.
NAHUM 1:2 KJV

Plenty of folks are perfectly willing to accept a wimpy kind of god—a perfectly inoffensive, powerless being who never interferes with their lives, never does anything *they* don't agree with, and *never* gets angry. This isn't God. Instead they've packed their own thinking in a little plastic doll, an idol created in their own image.

Imagine the anger any father would feel at having his son slighted! Well, God isn't just any father. He gave a unique Son. The perfect Man died to save sinners. To cost Your Son such pain and then receive the message "Don't interfere with my life" from sinners deserves an angry response. Justice wouldn't be done if God acted otherwise.

No idol shows anger, but God is no wimp. If people won't accept the most precious gift God had to give, they can pay for it themselves—with their own lives.

What will your life cost?

Father God, though I deserved wrath, You sent Your Son for me. I don't want to ignore His sacrifice.

PRAISE IN THE MIDST OF DOUBT

The Lord God is my strength, and he will make
my feet like hinds' feet, and he will make me
to walk upon mine high places.
HABAKKUK 3:19 KJV

Habakkuk had a hard time understanding God—Israel was a mess, and the Lord didn't seem to do anything about it. So the prophet went straight to the source to lodge his complaints—God Himself.

After a long conversation with Him, Habakkuk still didn't understand everything God was doing. The prophet didn't have all the answers, but he'd developed trust in God's sovereignty. The Creator was in control, and the prophet had faith again.

Even when you can't understand everything God is working out in your life, can you praise Him as sovereign Lord? Can you be confident in Him and climb to the mountaintop of belief?

If not, go to Him in prayer. Share your doubts and concerns, and give Him your burdens. Like Habakkuk, in a short while praise will overflow your heart.

Understanding all You do, Lord, is impossible. But I still trust that You are faithful. What I can't understand here, You can show me in heaven.

REBUILDING THE WALLS

Then I said to them, "You see the trouble
we are in: Jerusalem lies in ruins,
and its gates have been burned with fire.
Come, let us rebuild the wall of Jerusalem,
and we will no longer be in disgrace."
NEHEMIAH 2:17

Overcome with discouragement, the Jews who had returned to Jerusalem from exile huddled in a city open to invaders. Broken walls surrounded what was left of the city, and even its gates were burned. But no one started a citywide rebuilding project.

When Nehemiah heard of the situation, instead of hunkering down in fear, he got permission to rebuild the walls. He traveled to Jerusalem, inspected the site, and confronted the people. Encouragement and a plan were all the people needed—Nehemiah gave them both.

Sometimes every Christian needs lifting up. When job hunting gets you down, it's great to have someone show you the ropes and say something heartening. If you're struggling with sin, a seasoned Christian can share how she overcame the same temptation.

Don't let discouragement get the best of you. Reach out for help!

When I feel lower than a snake's navel, Lord, it's hard to tell others.
Help me reach out for help.

NEW LIFE

Therefore we are buried with him by baptism
unto death: that like as Christ was raised up
from the dead by the glory of the Father,
even so we also should walk
in newness of life.
ROMANS 6:4 KJV

You've been a Christian for a while, and that brand-new, clean feeling that came with a new faith has slowly evaporated.

Maybe, you ponder, *new is only for baby Christians. I know I've made "progress,"* you encourage yourself. *I'm not the same person I was before I knew Jesus.* But something's missing.

God didn't make Jesus new for a day, week, or month and then let Him get "old" again. He eternally raised Him from the dead, so through baptism we can share His new life forever.

If vibrant faith has left you, some "old" things probably tarnish your new life. Legalistic or critical attitudes, disobedience, and doubt take the shine off a once-new faith until you barely know you've been washed in the Lamb's blood.

But repentance during a let's-clear-the-air time with God returns the "new" to eternal life.

Spend time with Him in prayer.

Empty me of old things that keep me apart from You, Lord. I want to spend every new day close by Your side.

A True Friend

"Ye are my friends,
if ye do whatsoever I command you."
JOHN 15:14 KJV

Tina had more than her share of weddings in her future. Just after graduation, two friends were getting married. A week later, a cousin planned to say her vows, with Tina as maid of honor. By the end of June, Tina decided, her pockets would be empty.

But it wasn't the financial strain that bothered Tina. Her at-a-standstill romantic life was the real problem.

Three weddings, she thought, *and not a date for one of them.*

Tina wanted to share her friends' happiness, but being odd girl out hurt. It wouldn't have been so bad if there hadn't been *so many* weddings when she wasn't dating anyone.

Without even asking, Tina knew what Jesus wanted her to do. Shelving her own hurts, she went to the weddings and rejoiced in her friends' blessings. To her surprise, she had a great time and made a few new friends just because she didn't have a date!

Friendship with Jesus doesn't mean you'll always have a date—it means you'll always have a Friend.

When it's hard to obey Your commands, remind me, Friend, that I need to stick with You through the fun times and the tough ones.

THE WORLD OF DECISIONS

I have set before you life and death,
blessing and cursing: therefore choose life,
that both thou and thy seed may live:
That thou mayest love the Lord thy God,
and that thou mayest obey his voice,
and that thou mayest cleave unto him.

DEUTERONOMY 30:19–20 KJV

You're moving into a new life. As you graduate, a whole world sits out there to discover.

But it's a *big* world. Looking at the decisions you'll face and the things that could go wrong, you may feel scared.

Life's made up of a lot of decisions—do I move here, take that job, go along with the program or break away from it? More important, life is made up of moral choices that have even more impact on your future.

Bad moral choices can spell death for relationships, but good ones bring them new life. Choices close opportunities to you (after all, who wants to hire a thief?) or open up new vistas.

If you're really into the Word, you know what those right choices are. They're all in the Book. Put them to work in your life, and you'll be blessed!

When I read your Word, I see the things I should do. Give me strength, Lord, to follow through with right choices.

REACHING OUT TO OTHERS

"Therefore all things whatsoever ye would that
men should do to you, do ye even so to them:
for this is the law and the prophets."
MATTHEW 7:12 KJV

Jana sat in the crowded doctor's office, miserable with a head cold and barely paying attention to her surroundings. If only she could get in to see the doctor and get home and to bed!

She barely noticed the grimacing man across from her until another patient told the nurse, "He's in more pain than I am, please take him first."

Jana admired the woman, but guilt stabbed her heart. *I never realized he was in such pain,* she thought. *If I had, would I have done the same, even though it meant a longer wait?*

Doing good for others—especially those outside our circle of friends—means tuning in to their needs. Do we block ourselves behind a pseudospiritual wall and a "don't touch" mentality? Or do we open up to others, talk to hurting people, and offer them Jesus' help?

After all, that's only a small part of what He gave us.

Jesus, reaching out is hard when I get boxed into myself. Open my heart and eyes so I can help others.

STINKING FROGS. . .STINKING SIN

And the frogs died out of the houses,
out of the villages, and out of the fields.
And they gathered them together upon heaps:
and the land stank.
EXODUS 8:13–14 KJV

Pharaoh's sin stank in God's nose. So to let the ruler of Egypt know what it was like, God covered his land with dead, smelly frogs. No one in Egypt could get away from the putrid results of their ruler's disobedience. You might say it smelled to high heaven.

All Pharaoh had to do to end the plagues was let the Hebrew people go, but Egypt's ruler couldn't get the picture. Stuck in sin, he couldn't face the loss of his slaves. He backed out on his promise every time. The powerful ruler was the *real* slave.

When we're caught in sin, our wrongdoing reeks. God may not litter our houses with frogs, but somehow He lets us know. Take the Christian who complains constantly about the wrongs others do him and alienates all his friends. Because loneliness stinks, he'll start to listen to God and stop complaining.

Has your life gotten pretty stinky lately? Clean out the sin and breathe in fresh air.

Thank You, Jesus, for cleansing the sin from my life. Scour the filthy corners of my life so Your Spirit can freshen my soul.

A Picture of Jesus

And Joseph's ten brethren went down to buy corn in Egypt.
But Benjamin, Joseph's brother,
Jacob sent not with his brethren; for he said,
Lest peradventure mischief befall him.
GENESIS 42:3–4 KJV

Jacob might never have learned what happened the day Joseph disappeared, but he undoubtedly had some suspicions. Hadn't the favorite son died after he claimed he'd rule over his brothers? Jacob wasn't going to chance losing a second son.

Benjamin's ten brothers had earned themselves a reputation for being untrustworthy—and years after the incident, Jacob remembered it.

Getting a reputation isn't hard. People quickly judge your worth based on things you've done and what they've heard about you. Sometimes a reputation isn't deserved. But most often we've earned most of what we've gotten.

When people look at you, do they see something Jesus would be proud of? As a Christian, your reputation isn't just your own—it belongs to Jesus, too. People judge Him by your life.

I want others to see You in me, Lord, and I don't want to smudge the picture. Make me a trustworthy picture of Your love.

HEART TREASURE

Our holy and glorious temple,
where our fathers praised you,
has been burned with fire,
and all that we treasured lies in ruins.

ISAIAH 64:11

The Jews didn't have a place to worship. Their bright temple lay in ruins. Gone were the golden implements that made worship a pleasure. All they valued lay in ruins.

Come on! Were these guys crazy? What meant so much to them? Stones? Golden bowls and candlesticks? Fine woven hangings?

Or God?

Though their building was ruined, their relationship with God didn't have to be. They couldn't offer blood sacrifices, but God hadn't reneged on the promise of a Messiah who would save them. If only they had trusted Him! If they drew close to God, *He* could become a heart treasure that fire or war engines couldn't destroy and soldiers couldn't carry away.

If you've lost your church building or had to leave a congregation you love, don't let despair overwhelm you. God and His promises stand firm.

Make Him your treasure, and no one can turn your spiritual life to rubble.

Lord, be the treasure of my life. You're more than buildings or even a group of Christians. I'm part of Your eternal church, made up of those who love You.

LIFE ISN'T FAIR

And Joseph's master took him,
and put him into the prison,
a place where the king's prisoners were bound:
and he was there in the prison.
But the Lord was with Joseph, and shewed him mercy,
and gave him favour in the sight of the keeper of the prison.
GENESIS 39:20–21 KJV

Joseph didn't look for trouble—it just seemed to find him. First, his brothers sold him for a slave. Then his master's wife lied about him and got him tossed into prison.

If Joseph was favored by God so much, why wasn't his life smooth? we're tempted to ask. He didn't deserve what he got, especially not from Potiphar's wife.

The hard fact is that the wicked of this world don't live in a vacuum—they people the earth along with Christians, and sometimes Christians get hurt by their wrongdoing. When that happens, we cry out, "Life isn't fair!" And we're right, it isn't. But it wasn't fair, either, that Jesus had to come to earth for unbelievers and die to save them.

Are you ready to be treated unfairly for Him?

Lord, life isn't fair sometimes, but I still love You and want to serve You—even if it means getting mistreated by someone who doesn't know You.

SATAN'S DISGUISE

And no wonder, for Satan himself
masquerades as an angel of light.
It is not surprising, then, if his servants
masquerade as servants of righteousness.
2 CORINTHIANS 11:14–15

In certain circles, you'll hear a lot of false ideas about angels. People often use them as a more comfortable replacement for God—one that will supposedly tell them about the future, but won't demand anything from them.

When you hear ideas about angels that don't agree with Scripture, look out! Remember, not only are there heavenly beings, hellish beings seek to deceive us daily.

How can you tell the difference? Look at the message the messenger bears. God's angels constantly serve Him. They don't try to take His place or detract attention from Him. They bring glory to God, not themselves.

When Satan's messengers face us, they can look good. Who wouldn't want a personal heavenly being at his or her command? But pride isn't a key to heaven, and any being that encourages it doesn't come from there, either.

Lord, thank You for your angels who watch over us. But Satan's messengers I could do without. Keep me from the pride that hides truth from my eyes.

TRUST GOD AS YOUR GUIDE

Finally, brethren, whatsoever things are true,
whatsoever things are honest,
whatsoever things are just,
whatsoever things are pure,
whatsoever things are lovely,
whatsoever things are of good report;
if there be any virtue,
and if there be any praise,
think on these things.
PHILIPPIANS 4:8 KJV

If you don't have a job yet, this *isn't* the time to spend your days in front of soap operas. They'll only make you depressed, with their tales of scheming and sin.

It's hard not to know where life's leading you, and negatives can easily permeate your thoughts. Doubts assail your mind when you don't have a clear-cut future. But when job-hunter's depression hangs over you, spend some *serious* time in prayer. You may not hear a voice from heaven say, "Here's the job, in this company, at this pay," but assurance that God is working for you will fill your heart. Hang on to that assurance when Satan tosses questions in your mind!

Don't give in to negative thinking. Instead search out positives and focus on them. Spend a few hours in the evening doing things you enjoy and that lift your spirits.

But most of all, trust the God who made you to guide you in the right path.

When I don't know where I'm going, Lord, I can still hang on to You. Show me the way.

HONOUR THY FATHER AND THY MOTHER

Honour thy father and thy mother,
as the Lord thy God hath commanded thee.
DEUTERONOMY 5:16 KJV

Since I moved out, my mom constantly calls me. Then the other day she dropped in and cleaned my apartment because she didn't think I'd done a good job. She thought she was doing me a favor, but I'm furious," Carla admitted.

You're stepping out, gaining independence, but Mom and Dad don't want to let go. Though you don't want to treat your parents disrespectfully, you *are* on your own. Ten years from now, you don't want Mom stopping by to clean!

Carla's mom didn't care so much how clean Carla's place was. She *really* wanted to spend time with her daughter, but when conversation lagged, Mom felt uncomfortable and started dusting. Once Carla discovered that, an occasional phone call let Mom know she was still loved. They met for lunch once in a while, and the relationship blossomed.

You can honor your parents without doing everything the way they do. Just treat them with respect and keep on loving them.

Lord, when my parents and I disagree, keep us communicating. I want to honor You and them.

DEEPER BEAUTY

Whose adorning let it not be that outward adorning of
plaiting the hair, and of wearing of gold,
or of putting on of apparel;
But let it be the hidden man of the heart,
in that which is not corruptible,
even the ornament of a meek and quiet spirit,
which is in the sight of God of great price.
1 PETER 3:3–4 KJV

Some people would look great dressed in anything, with no makeup. The rest of us need a little help—and there's nothing wrong with looking your best. A few hours a week in the gym will not only tighten up your waistline but also leave you healthier and happier. A new dress or suit may make you more confident.

On the other hand, we all know perfectly gorgeous people whose souls live in a swamp. You may admire their appearance but wouldn't trust them to walk your dog. Their beauty is skin deep—or less.

In the long run, it's performance that counts, which is exactly what this verse is saying. Do the best that you can with your outer self, but concentrate on the "unfading beauty of a gentle and quiet spirit."

Lord, I will never be one of the beautiful people the world seems to favor, but I can develop the kind of inner beauty that You prefer. Thank You for judging me on the basis of how I live, not how I look.

BUILDING A GODLY NATION

Blessed is the nation whose God is the Lord.
PSALM 33:12

We don't have a state religion because our forefathers who lived under them experienced them as oppressive, limiting individual freedom. While it might be efficient to have one religion for all, we just won't line up like sheep going through a gate. It's not in our character. We're a nation of fence jumpers.

Were our forefathers great examples of godliness? Probably not. They broke the same commandments we do, just as often as we do. The fact that the press didn't follow them around with a telephoto lens probably helped their reputation, though.

It would be inaccurate to say that our country follows the Lord God today and is blessed because of it. As a political unit, it doesn't, but as individuals, we can. Those who prize religious freedom are still free to be as good as they can be, to apply religious principles to their own lives anytime they want to, and to build a nation where the Lord God is free to reign in *their* hearts.

Father, thank You for the many freedoms we enjoy in this country. Help us build a righteous nation, one person at a time.

A CHANGE OF PLANS

"For I know the plans I have for you,"
says the Lord. "They are plans for good and not
for disaster, to give you a future and a hope."
JEREMIAH 29:11 NLT

We all have plans for our future, even if they're a little vague. We know whether we want to marry and have children, places we want to go, and things we hope to accomplish. Most of us are realistic about our plans, knowing some will work out and some won't. We also know our plans will change from year to year as we mature and see more of the world.

What we don't like is to have our plans blown out of the water and to have our lives take a sudden change of direction. There's nothing more frightening than losing the anchor that's been holding our life in place and being forced to start over again.

Fortunately, some of these disasters turn out to be blessings. Even when we have no idea which way to turn, the Lord knows where we're going and will keep us on the right path, even if the trip's a little bumpy.

Father, when my life suddenly turns upside down, I will trust in You to lead me in the right direction.

DREAMS AND FANTASIES

He who works his land
will have abundant food,
but the one who chases fantasies
will have his fill of poverty.
PROVERBS 28:19

Two or three generations ago, young people were advised, "Learn a trade and you'll always have work." This was during the depression, and the advice was good, just as the verse above is good advice. Society changes, and the available jobs change with it. Today it's a good idea to know your way around the Internet and a computer keyboard. Who knows what new jobs will open up in the next twenty years?

All vocational advice is based on the same premise: Pick a job, do it well, and don't chase fantasies. This doesn't mean you shouldn't dream of a better job, but it should be a realistic dream, attainable through education or experience.

Go ahead and dream, but back your dream up with productive work, just in case.

Lord, I have so many dreams and hopes. Some will come true and some won't. Teach me the difference between dreams and fantasies and lead me into the work You have designed for me.

THE HOLY ONE AMONG US

For I am God, and not man;
the Holy One in the midst of thee.
HOSEA 11:9 KJV

We have to be careful not to confuse human beings with God. Humanity was made in God's image, but we're only a tiny little reflection of all He is. We see our limits every day and tend to apply them to God. It's a perfectly human thing to do, although inaccurate.

We tend to give God human characteristics. When nature devastates part of the world, we think God must be angry at someone. When a great discovery brings a company wealth, we say God is pleased with the company. Bad things happen to good people; good things happen to the evil. How can we say God is wrong in either case?

The Holy One among us is God, not human. Sometimes He is a mystery to us, and we might as well admit that and stop trying to make Him more like ourselves.

Father, I cannot begin to imagine Your glory and power. Be patient when I limit You in my mind.

JUDGMENT BELONGS TO GOD

You, then, why do you judge your brother?
Or why do you look down on your brother?
For we will all stand before
God's judgment seat.
ROMANS 14:10

Are you absolutely sure you know the mind of God? Can you judge others on the basis of what you know today? More important, whom do *you* want to be judged by? Look at our court system, where the guilty often go free and the innocent suffer. Would you trust that system with your ultimate judgment?

Yet we go on judging others every day of our lives. We do have to make some important choices. Some people we don't want to associate with for one reason or another, so to a certain extent, we do have to judge. Where we get into trouble is when we condemn. It's one thing to avoid someone whose actions we disapprove of, but condemning him or her is something else. We aren't equipped for that job, since no one knows the full story of another's life. "Do not condemn, and you will not be condemned" (Luke 6:37).

Father, help me in the daily choices I must make, but remind me that judgment is Yours to administer, not mine.

TEMPTATIONS ARE NOT FROM GOD

When tempted, no one should say,
"God is tempting me."
For God cannot be tempted by evil,
nor does he tempt anyone.
JAMES 1:13

In other words, Flip Wilson was right when he said, "The devil made me do it," although he was just using the devil to excuse his own actions.

We're all tempted now and then, and when we are, we try to blame someone else. Sometimes we blame another human, our own human weaknesses, the devil, or even God. But God *never* tempts anyone. At the most, He might allow us to be tempted by someone else, but other than taking this hands-off approach, He is blameless.

It's not that God is unable to tempt us. There's no doubt He could do a bang-up job of it, if He wanted to, but He doesn't. So when you goof up, don't place the blame in the wrong place. Most of the time, you did yourself in.

God will not tempt you, but He will help when others do, so before you go ahead and make the wrong choice, ask for His help, which He gives freely and with love.

Father, thank You for Your care and love, which will enable me to resist the temptations that come my way.

CREDIT CARDS

Owe no man any thing.
ROMANS 13:8 KJV

How many credit cards did you receive in the mail before you graduated? Banks routinely send shiny new cards out to seniors, all "preapproved." Just sign the form and you're an adult, often before you have a job. Sure, the credit limit is pretty low, but in a year or so it will be mysteriously raised to a level you can't possibly afford.

Your first credit card is a rite of passage. Someone actually trusts you to pay your bills! And it's certainly handy. So accept one of the many offered if you feel you need it, but don't fall into the trap of accepting five or six of them, or you'll never be able to pay them all off when the bills come in.

If you can't pay a credit card bill in full when it's due, you shouldn't be using a card at all. A fistful of fully loaded cards, paid off with minimum monthly payments, will never have a zero balance. You don't need that. You could take the interest you will have to pay, invest it in a mutual fund, and double your money before your credit card will be paid off. It's better to do without than to fall into the credit trap.

Father, teach me how to handle my money wisely and not spend more than I earn at this stage of my life.

THE SIN PROBLEM

I do not understand what I do.
For what I want to do I do not do,
but what I hate I do.
ROMANS 7:15

Paul was as human as the rest of us and not afraid to admit it. "I don't know why I act the way I do," he said. "I don't do the things I want to do. Instead, I do what I don't want to do."

We don't know what Paul's sins were, but they really bugged him, and it seems he never conquered them, although he obviously worked on them a lot. His standards for himself were probably pretty high.

You set yourself up to fail if you think you should be perfect. Are you better than Paul was? Have a little mercy on yourself.

This doesn't mean you should use Paul's failure as an excuse to run wild or not even try to control yourself. Paul conquered a good portion of his weaknesses, and you can do the same. Pick out one of your least-favorite behaviors and concentrate on it for a while. You may be surprised—but don't expect perfection.

Lord, my sins are numerous and my strengths are few. Help me be the best I can be and trust Your forgiveness for the rest.

Unfailing Love

Unto Adam also and to his wife did the Lord
God make coats of skins, and clothed them.
GENESIS 3:21 KJV

This verse comes right after God cursed Adam and Eve and right before He chased them out of Eden. Smack dab in the middle of all the thundering and armed angels, God took some animal skins and did a little sewing. What's going on here?

Well, that's parenting for you. How many times did your mom yell at you, then turn around and bake cookies before she finished her lecture? How many times did your father tell you to be more careful with your money and then hand you a twenty before he told you what *not* to spend it on?

The next time you're ready to blow up at someone, follow God's example. Take a break. Do a little something to show you care for the person, and let your love defuse your anger.

Father, thank You for Your unfailing love when I goof up. Your anger would be more than I could stand.

THE RAINS WILL COME

See how the farmer waits for the land
to yield its valuable crop
and how patient he is for
the autumn and spring rains.
JAMES 5:7

If there's one thing a farmer knows well, it's patience. You can't hurry a plant's growth, and you can't do a thing to bring the rain. Standing in the field and looking at the sky is often all that can be done.

It's hard to be patient in an instant world. You need to shake off that cold right now, but your nose is still going to run for five days unless you take so much medicine you can't function. A baby comes when it comes, conveniently or not. The puppy will be housebroken when it decides to be, so don't buy a new rug yet. Nature has a way of telling us we're not the hotshots we think we are.

We have to remember that although we can control a lot of our life, there's a lot more we can't do anything about, and there's no sense in getting upset about what we can't control. The rains will come.

Father, teach me patience when I'm faced with something I cannot control. There is enough that I can work on to keep me busy until the time is right.

PERSEVERANCE

Perseverance must finish its work
so that you may be mature and complete,
not lacking anything.
JAMES 1:4

We don't often think of perseverance as a blessing or something beneficial to our growth. We persevere because the only other options are defeat or retreat. We don't go out looking for the chance to persevere; it usually involves unpleasant experiences.

Whether or not we want these experiences, they will come. The requirements of our job may be beyond our capabilities, yet we persevere and eventually learn how to handle the work. Losing the twenty pounds we put on at college seems to go on forever, yet we lose a little every week and eventually get there.

Perseverance is tiny little steps toward a goal, not one valiant effort that solves the problem immediately. It teaches patience, planning, and working for future rewards instead of instant gratification—all things that lead to maturity and completeness.

Father, perseverance is hard work, no matter what the goal is. Give me the patience and foresight I need to persevere and mature.

LEARNING TO LISTEN

Rejoice with those who rejoice;
mourn with those who mourn.
ROMANS 12:15

Have you noticed how short our attention span has become? Our movies have to have constant action. The same thing goes for books: Don't bother to show us the setting unless someone's lurking in the shadows. Life's too short for character development.

We do the same thing in our personal relationships. Listening is a lost art. Now when we're silent it's because we're waiting our turn to speak, not listening to what the other person is saying. As a result, the only person we truly relate to is ourselves.

That's not what friendship is supposed to be like. It takes time and patience to be a friend. You have to really listen, because often real feelings come out slowly, a bit at a time. How can you rejoice with someone when you have no idea what makes him happy? How can you mourn with a friend when you never knew her mother was dying?

Try being a good listener for a few months and watch your circle of friends expand. You'll never be alone in a crowd again.

Father, teach me to be a good listener, someone with the patience to hear a story to its end and really try to understand.

TAKING CHANCES

Sometimes we are our own worst enemies. We run away from so many things that frighten us, trusting our fears more than the Lord who protects and shelters us.

Some fear commitment so much that they drive away those they love. Others are so worried about money that they never enjoy anything without first checking the price tag. Fear of losing a job keeps some from showing any initiative or creativity, which in itself can endanger their jobs.

The world is full of fearsome things, and a certain amount of caution is required, but there's no reason to let fear run our lives. Maturity and achievement come to those who know how to take a few chances. Sometimes you get bitten by a strange dog; most of the time, he licks your hand.

Trust the Lord with your life and step out in courage and strength.

Father, thank You for Your love and care every day of my life. Help me trust You for my safety, which will let me live in quietness and strength.

KEEPING PROMISES

I will pay that that I have vowed.
JONAH 2:9 KJV

Jonah proved that welshing on a promise made to God is a bad idea. He tried to run away from such a promise and almost died before he changed his mind (admittedly under pressure) and renewed his vow. Fortunately, this time he kept his word.

Yet we go on making promises to God today and breaking them tomorrow. We also break the promises we make to others. In neither case are we tossed off boats and saved by sea creatures, but you have to believe that God's not exactly pleased by our failures.

Promises should never be taken lightly. You can break a person's heart by breaking a promise. You can lose a job, be drummed out of military service, or never be trusted again. Never promise more than you can deliver.

Father, make me think before I promise anything to anyone. If I can't keep a promise, I should never make it in the first place.

GOD'S TASKS

Keep your servant also from willful sins;
may they not rule over me.

PSALM 19:13

B ecause you're a Christian, you want to serve Jesus. He saved you from so much, and you're grateful. Why, if you could give Him the whole world, it wouldn't be enough.

What if He asked you to give up your car, career, or girlfriend? Would you still be keen to serve? A lot of Christians wouldn't be.

We say we want to serve Jesus, but do we? Do we tell Him we'll witness, but we won't talk to our friends? Do we want to serve only behind the scenes and never give a testimony?

Only willful servants identify the gifts they feel comfortable with and try to make God use them. Real servants take the place He commands.

Witnessing to friends or giving a public testimony may seem impossible. *I could never do that*, you may think.

Alone, you probably never would. But you don't have to rely on yourself. You can rely on Him to enable you to do anything He calls you to do.

Today God may call you to serve in areas that seem nearly impossible. If so, take on that task. When it looks most impossible, His grace will be at hand.

Set your tasks before me, Your servant, Lord. I know Your enabling power will come.

GOD'S CHOICE

And they prayed, and said,
Thou, Lord, which knowest the hearts of all men,
shew whether of these two thou hast chosen,
That he may take part of this ministry and
apostleship, from which Judas by transgression
fell, that he might go to his own place.
ACTS 1:24–25 KJV

Peter and the other apostles knew God's promises. Two Scriptures implied that Judas's place should be filled. So they shopped around, found two likely replacements, prayed that God would chose between *their* two choices, and filled the spot with Matthias.

Scripture never again mentions Matthias.

Those well-meaning apostles had rushed to fill the empty slot in their "church board" and chose the wrong man.

How could they have chosen the right one? Saul, Christian persecutor, hardly seemed to fit the bill.

It took time—and God's timing—to make Saul into an apostle. He had to come face to face with Jesus and experience conversion. The "new man," Paul, was the perfect person to bring the Gospel to a tough bunch of Gentiles.

Like Peter and his friends, we often rush to do "God's work" in our way.

Have you prayed *and* waited for God's answer?

I want to obey You, Jesus. Show me Your plan, not my own.

GOD'S FAITHFULNESS

" 'I am with you and will save you,' "
declares the Lord. 'Though I completely destroy
all the nations among which I scatter you,
I will not completely destroy you.' "
JEREMIAH 30:11

*B*abylon. Not a name you read in the *New York Times. U.S. News & World Report* doesn't mention it, either.

Why? Because Babylon fell centuries ago. Pass over it in history class, and it *is* history. You'll never hear about that country in the news.

But you'll read all about Israel.

God promised the Jews who were facing exile in Babylon that He'd never destroy them. Then the Lord split up His people, sending them as slaves into a foreign land. Years later, their conquering country, Babylon, fell, but conquered Israel returned to life.

Israel didn't always exist as a nation. For centuries, Jews were spread all over the world, with no homeland. But God hadn't deserted the people whom He'd called to Himself. He promised to bring her back, and in 1948, He did.

God remained faithful to a promise He made to a rebellious people He was punishing for their sin. Will He be less faithful to you?

Imagine the promises one *faithful* person could see Him fulfill!

Faithfulness like Yours, Lord, amazes me. Even when I fail You, You don't desert me. Keep me faithful to You today.

THE TESTIMONY

For ye have heard of my conversation
in time past in the Jews' religion,
how that beyond measure I persecuted
the church of God, and wasted it.
GALATIANS 1:13 KJV

Before becoming a Christian, Bette had been sexually involved with a number of guys, and people knew it.

Once she knew God, Bette struggled with that sin and began to gain victory over it.

But when her youth group wanted to start an outreach to her classmates, Bette balked at the idea of helping out. "You don't understand; I have a reputation there. It makes no difference that I'm a Christian. Plenty of people still point a finger at me."

Her pastor, knowing how much Bette had changed, still wanted her to give her testimony. "It will be a challenge," he admitted. "But I think you can take it on. You can't run away from the past, so tell people about it. You have a great testimony to share."

If you have an embarrassing past that you've gained victory over, don't fear it. Paul had one, too. Instead of hiding his persecution of the church, he let God use it to bring Him glory.

Some may have pointed, but more believed.

Lord, You've worked a miracle in my life. Don't let me be shy in sharing what You've done.

A HEART PROBLEM

They are darkened in their understanding
and separated from the life of God
because of the ignorance that is in them
due to the hardening of their hearts.
EPHESIANS 4:18

Ross didn't know how many times he and Kevin had talked about the world's beginning, the environment, and recent scientific discoveries. But their discussions always reached an impasse. No matter how clear his arguments were, Ross felt his friend just wouldn't accept them. Instead Kevin held fast to a few illogical beliefs, no matter how hard Ross tried to show him how wrong they were.

Showing a non-Christian how wrong he is can be a deadly witnessing tool. It rarely works, because, like Kevin, he'll become defensive. Then you don't have a chance to discover the real objections.

Kevin's problem wasn't really with the world. Years ago he had decided he didn't believe in God, who didn't seem to answer one childhood prayer. All Ross's logic didn't deal with that heartfelt issue.

Have a friend with a heart problem? Don't try to convince him. Instead pray for him and show him Jesus' love until his heart is opened.

Lord, soften the hearts of my non-Christian friends and family members. Work in Your Spirit where I can't touch.

CAUGHT IN THE MIDDLE

And Hushai said unto Absalom, Nay;
but whom the Lord, and this people,
and all the men of Israel, choose, his will I be,
and with him will I abide. And again,
whom should I serve? should I not serve in the
presence of his son? as I have served in thy
father's presence, so will I be in thy presence.
2 SAMUEL 16:18–19 KJV

Hushai got caught right in the middle of a political war between King David and his son Absalom. Because he needed information on his son's doings, David asked his friend to stay in Jerusalem after Absalom took over. So Hushai became David's inside man in Jerusalem.

Despite his dangerous position, Hushai spoke the truth to would-be-king Absalom. Up front he said he'd serve the one God had chosen. Was it Hushai's fault that David's proud son thought that was *him?* Hushai *did* serve Absalom by giving him the truth.

Hushai was in a position much like the corporate worker who tells his boss the truth he doesn't want to hear. It was right, but it wouldn't make him popular.

If the falsehoods of office politics threaten you, stand firm, like Hushai. You'll be serving One even greater than your boss.

Lord, I don't want office politics to blind me to Your will. Keep me in Your truth.

JONAH'S POUT

I do well to be angry, even unto death.
JONAH 4:9 KJV

Sometimes God does something we really don't like. Perhaps a friend's mom dies or a cousin's girl jilts him. It doesn't seem right, and anger fills us. *How could You do this?* we ask, forgetting—or ignoring—that He is Lord of the universe.

Jonah had seen his nation's enemies coming to God. It didn't seem fair, and Jonah flew into a snit. In fact, he was so mad, he wanted to perish.

Anger often attacks when we feel helpless about our situation. We can't imagine things changing this way, and we hate it, so we want out. Death looks better than staying here and putting up with it.

But where would death have gotten the prophet? Would it have changed what God had done or helped Israel?

No.

We can lose ourselves in anger or trust that God is still good and still in control. After all, the changes of a day can't alter the truth of eternity.

Lord, I don't always understand the way You work. But I need to trust in You anyway. Help me to keep my eyes on You, not my own "should-be" plans.

LITTLE FOXES

Catch for us the foxes,
the little foxes that ruin the vineyards,
our vineyards that are in bloom.
SONG OF SONGS 2:15

L eave your dirty dishes overnight, and what could have been an easy cleaning job becomes a crusty, dried-on mess. Don't do them in the morning, and their smell could soon drive you from your home.

Sin is like those dishes. Deal with it when you first notice it in your life, and it doesn't get ingrained. You confess it to God, turn away from it quickly, and like the little fox mentioned in Song of Songs, it won't become a big fox that ruins the fruit in your spiritual vineyard.

Ignore sin until it has a real hold on you, and your vines start dying.

Are you bearing a grudge, ignoring a task God has set before you, or losing sight of your daily walk with God? Act today. Move that little fox out of your spiritual life and into the forest, where it belongs.

Lord, I don't want sin growing in my life instead of Your fruit of the Spirit. Rid me of unforgiven sin.

OPEN WITNESSES

Then came the Jews round about him,
and said unto him...
If thou be the Christ, tell us plainly.
Jesus answered them, "I told you,
and ye believed not: the works that I do
in my Father's name, they bear witness of me.
But ye believe not, because ye are not of my sheep."
JOHN 10:24–26 KJV

Some confused Jews wanted Jesus to say, "I am the Messiah," because they thought it would end their doubts.

Though Jesus didn't say those words, He pointed out that you know a person by what he or she does.

Jesus had taught in the streets and countryside about the Father, lived out in the open, where people could see His testimony, and healed publicly. People saw who He was and what He did.

Whether or not they liked it was another matter.

We live out our Christian testimony publicly, too. We can't act like Goody Two-shoes in church but commit sin privately and not have it subtly destroy our witness.

An honest testimony may convict unbelievers—or they may remain unconverted because of unbelief. Jesus didn't convince everyone He spoke to, and neither will we.

We're open witnesses, not conscience keepers.

Lord Jesus, I want my public testimony to reflect my private faith.
Today I want people to see what You can do in my life.

THE MIRROR

Anyone who listens to the word
but does not do what it says is like a man
who looks at his face in a mirror and,
after looking at himself, goes away
and immediately forgets what he looks like.
JAMES 1:23–24

Scripture gives us a mirror-image picture of ourselves. Sometimes, when that view's sin filled, we'd like to smash the mirror that shows us our true selves.

Those hard-to-face-up-to Bible passages show us our sin. We know we need to change our ways and struggle with that need. So we read the Word, even talk about it with other Christians, verbally agree to what it says, then turn our backs on it. We don't put the Word into action because we can't wait to lose our pain.

James compares turning our backs to forgetting what we look like. Disregarding the sin doesn't change our "face." God sees it; other people perceive it. We only fool ourselves.

When you see sin in the mirror, turn to God for forgiveness and healing. Only He can give you a new "face."

I'd rather walk a thousand miles than face up to sin, Lord. But start
me on the pilgrimage that makes me clean and fit for You.

My Hope Is Jesus

Thou, O Lord, remainest for ever;
thy throne from generation to generation.
LAMENTATIONS 5:19 KJV

For verses, Jeremiah's been crying the blues about the destruction of Jerusalem. How can he suddenly write something like this?

Judah's situation was about as bad as it could get. Conquered by Babylon, Jeremiah's nation had been wiped out, her best people carted off into exile. Those who hadn't been killed or carried away were scrounging for food.

Pretty grim.

The prophet felt despondent, but he still knew whom he could turn to. God was their only hope, even if He took His time answering Jeremiah's prayer.

Sometimes life gets hopeless. The person you thought you'd marry says good-bye. A family member is dangerously ill. The job you thought you'd done so well at disappears.

But you still have hope. His name is Jesus, and He'll answer your prayers right on schedule.

Lord, when You don't answer my prayers the way I want, help me to keep trusting in You. What else can give me hope when life looks grim?

RESOLVING CONFLICT

Before certain men came from James,
he [Peter] used to eat with the Gentiles.
But when they arrived,
he began to draw back and separate himself from
the Gentiles because he was afraid of those who
belonged to the circumcision group.

GALATIANS 2:12

Paul had a problem with Brother Peter. Peter had taken a stand for the Gentiles, but when that stand seemed unpopular, he backed down.

Probably, Paul's irritation partly stemmed from his soft spot for the Gentiles, but even more, the apostle was upset at Peter's misunderstanding of the Gospel. Faith in Jesus mattered, not rules and regulations.

Unlike many Christians, Paul didn't pass his displeasure on to the rest of the church first. He simply confronted Peter. This may not have been the first time they'd discussed the issue, since other Christians were on hand to hear them out.

When you disagree with a church member, do you follow Paul's plan for discussion and resolution? Or do you talk to everyone *except* the offender?

Paul and Peter's serious division would influence all Christianity, not just themselves. But they worked it out in love.

You can do it, too.

Lord, I want to resolve conflict in the church, not add to it. Give me the courage to gently confront the one I disagree with.

THE FOOLISHNESS OF PRIDE

When pride cometh, then cometh shame:
but with the lowly is wisdom.
PROVERBS 11:2 KJV

In a single century we've gone from horse-and-buggy days to outer space. What scientific progress we've made.

But even the greatest scientific discovery hasn't found a cure for pride. If anything, our age of discovery has fueled our own arrogance. It's not uncommon for late twentieth-century people to look down on those from long ago. *How much more we know*, we think. *How ignorant they were.*

Such thinking disregards the fact that ancient Egyptians built pyramids using sophisticated techniques we can only guess at. People back then weren't so dumb.

Is it so hard to believe that the Messiah described by David, Isaiah, and other prophets could be real? These men weren't stupid, either; they just lived in a different time.

When people try to tell you the Bible can't be true, that its writers lived too long ago to know anything, understand that you're listening to human pride.

Turn to Jesus for the truth instead.

Lord, I don't want to get bound up in pride. Show me the light of Your truth.

PAID IN FULL

He forgave us all our sins,
having canceled the written code,
with its regulations,
that was against us and that stood opposed to us;
he took it away, nailing it to the cross.
COLOSSIANS 2:13–14

C redit card bills can be such stinkers—especially if you watch them skyrocket. Pay only the minimum balance, and that debt is yours forever.

What if you got a call from your credit card company one day saying, "Because you're our customer, we're canceling all your debt. We felt compassionate today"?

You'd probably go to a doctor to get your hearing checked. Or a psychiatrist to see if you were all right from the neck up. People don't just forgive business debts.

Paul describes sin as a business debt, with strict rules and regulations about payment and penalties.

On the cross, Jesus paid your ever-increasing debt and fulfilled those rules and regulations. At the same time He paid a perfect price for a valueless object—sin.

He did that because He loves you.

Can you ever feel valueless again?

Lord, You gave Your life for all my empty sin and made my life valuable again. Thank You for such love.

THE BLESSING OF FAITH

But Thomas, one of the twelve,
called Didymus. . .said unto them,
Except I shall see in his hands the print of the nails, . . .
and thrust my hand into his side,
I will not believe."
JOHN 20:24–25 KJV

How hard it must have been for Thomas Didymus, the Twin. Inside his mind, he had two poles. One said faith, the other, reason. No matter what the issue, he was pulled from side to side.

When the disciples told him they'd seen Jesus, Thomas sided with reason. Though he knew Peter, John, and the others weren't the lying sort, their report seemed unbelievable. Giving it credence would take a lot of blind faith, and Thomas wasn't going to be blind.

Thomas finally ended his battle between faith and reason with the words, "My Lord and my God" (v. 28), but only after seeing was believing. Reason had to be balanced equally with faith until Thomas saw Jesus and recognized Him as God.

Are you waiting to see things God wants you to trust by faith? You'll be missing the blessing of faith.

Jesus, I don't want a divided faith. Make me whole and strong in belief in You today.

GOD SEES ALL

Good deeds are obvious,
and even those that are not cannot be hidden.
1 TIMOTHY 5:25

Some of our good deeds are obvious to everyone. If you regularly show up to do volunteer work, you will develop a reputation as a faithful worker. If you treat your parents with respect, the neighborhood will call you a good son or daughter. You don't do these things to impress others, but it's nice to be recognized as a good person.

Many of your good deeds will not be noticed by others, however, and you won't receive any praise for doing them. In fact, some may gain you nothing but trouble.

But that doesn't mean you should give up. Your concern and care may not be noticed or trusted, but God sees and remembers every good deed you do.

Father, it's hard to be distrusted when I know I am just trying to help. Sometimes I'm tempted to be as cynical as everyone else. When I'm hurt by someone's response to my good intentions, reassure me that I'm behaving the way You want me to.

PEACEMAKERS

"Blessed are the peacemakers:
for they shall be called the children of God."
MATTHEW 5:9 KJV

Have you ever found yourself in the middle of a family argument? Maybe your dad and brother are at odds over some issue, and you step in to try to bring them back together. You offer what you think is a reasonable compromise, only to have both of them tell you to butt out and mind your own business. Often the two of them will join forces and turn on you. Well, that's one problem solved—and another begun.

The problem with being a peacemaker is that you can't totally please both sides. They don't want to come to an agreement; they want to win! So what do you do, give up? Let them fight it out on their own? In some cases, you can do just that, but in others the stakes are too high, and you'll just have to accept the fact that both sides may end up hating you for the time being when you try to be a peacemaker. It isn't easy being a child of God.

Father, give me the courage to be a peacemaker when I can help and the good sense to know when my efforts will be useless. I want to do Your will, whatever the cost.

LEARNING WHO TO TRUST

Continue in what you have learned
and have become convinced of,
because you know those from
whom you learned it.
2 TIMOTHY 3:14

I t's always a good idea to know who is teaching you what. A lot of us learn from the media. Modern communication is a wonderful tool, but do you know what the commentator believes and how that may influence him to skew his report one way or another? Do you take the time to really look into issues for yourself, or do you just take someone's word for what's going on?

Before you swallow something whole, look at it carefully. Does it agree with what you believe in? Have teachers you trust said the same thing about this issue? Can you see a hidden agenda there that someone hopes you will miss? Until proven otherwise, it's a good idea to trust your old, familiar teachers instead of those you do not know at all.

Father, teach me discernment in what I believe and trust in. I need to learn to make up my own mind, not blindly follow the leading of others.

How We Live; Not Where We Live

Blessed shalt thou be in the city,
and blessed shalt thou be in the field.
DEUTERONOMY 28:3 KJV

People get locked into mental mindsets that can strongly affect the way they look at life. Those who live in great cities consider anyone living elsewhere as hicks, narrow-minded and somewhat slow, both physically and mentally. Those living in small towns think all city dwellers are heart-less, cold, and narrow-minded. City folk transformed into countryfolk say they are never accepted in their new homes, while those who move from the country to the city say the exact same thing.

Nothing is ever going to change this. We can always find someone to look down on; and even though the Bible warns us not to act this way, it still goes on.

What we continue to forget is that God really doesn't care where we live. To Him, it's how we live that counts, and we can live a blessed life anywhere we want to. Good people can live in cities or towns; bad people can live on farms or in con-dos. It's not the place that counts, it's the hearts living there.

Father, teach me not to judge people on the basis of where they live, but accept everyone as a potential child of God.

LAUGHTER AND TEARS

Even in laughter the heart may ache,
and joy may end in grief.
PROVERBS 14:13

You probably know the story of the clown who managed to keep on laughing although his heart was breaking. He had a job to do, no matter how he felt personally, so he did it. Depending on your point of view, you can think of that clown as a hero or a fool, but either way he put others before himself.

Laughter and tears are close relatives. We can laugh so hard it brings tears to our eyes, and sometimes we find ourselves laughing in an unconscious attempt to cope with intense sorrow. More than a few people have been struck with the giggles during a funeral. It's embarrassing and inappropriate, but it's just another human reaction to grief.

We can never predict how someone will handle strong emotions, and we certainly should not judge anyone on the basis of how they handle their emotions under stress.

Father, I realize not everyone has a firm grip on their emotions and I should never be too hasty to condemn someone's reaction to a stressful event. Help me give the support that is needed, whether it's tears or laughter.

GOOD ADVICE

Plans succeed through good counsel.
PROVERBS 20:18 NLT

If you graduated last spring, you've probably had all the advice you want for a while. Parents, grandparents, teachers, pastors, and guidance counselors have been telling you what to do for the last twenty years. It's time for you to make your own plans.

You're right. You probably are ready to do your own thing. No one wants you to come running for help with every little decision. You have to make your own choices and live with the results.

That doesn't mean you won't still want some selective advice, though. This time you will seek it out, instead of having others determine what you need to know. The initiative is yours now. If you have a little money to invest, you can find your own financial advisor. A friend can tell you about a good doctor or dentist. A mentor at work can advise you on how to get ahead. The advice you seek out yourself can be even more valuable than the advice someone pushes on you without asking if you want it.

Father, help me find the advice I need to make my plans work out. I don't know everything, and I do need to know the questions I should be asking.

THE LEARNING CHALLENGE

Apply your heart to instruction
and your ears to words of knowledge.
PROVERBS 23:12

Everyone looks back on high school and college days as days of carefree fun. Of course that's because additional cares and responsibilities follow the school years, and sometimes catching the 7:00 A.M. train makes sitting in a classroom seem like a piece of cake.

The truth is, learning is hard work. It's not half as carefree as we remember it being. Names, dates, equations, philosophies, term papers, and unreasonably high grade curves give students a lot of grief. All that knowledge doesn't just flow into your brain and stick. If you're juggling coursework for a higher degree with work responsibilities, you're probably realizing that fact all over again.

Don't be discouraged, though. No matter what challenges life brings you, your heavenly Father is always by your side, waiting to help you out.

Father, remind me today that nothing is too hard for me when You are by my side.

GOD IS MY REFUGE

The eternal God is thy refuge,
and underneath are the everlasting arms.
DEUTERONOMY 33:27 KJV

Sometimes we think of God as an avenger, punisher, and slayer of the unrighteous—someone we'd better not cross. The Old Testament, read too hastily, often gives us that idea, with all its curses, fires, destroyed nations.

And yet, right there in Deuteronomy is this verse, with its loving promise. God is also our refuge, the one we can always run to. He protects us from bullies, just like our big brother did. He kisses our wounds and makes them better, like Mom. He opens His arms—His *everlasting* arms—and protects us from those who would hurt us, just like Dad.

Whenever we're far from home, struggling to make our way in a cutthroat world, God will be there for us. He's never too busy to help. His lap is never too full for one more lost kid. He never fails to comfort and protect.

We don't deserve this much love. We can't even begin to imagine it. And yet it's there for us anytime we need it.

Father, thank You for letting me climb into Your everlasting arms anytime I need to, for saving my life anytime it needs it, for being my Father.

THE ANGELS IN OUR LIVES

For he will command his angels concerning
you to guard you in all your ways;
they will lift you up in their hands,
so that you will not strike your foot against a stone.
PSALM 91:11–12

Your mother or grandmother probably told you about your guardian angel when you were young and afraid to look under your bed at night, but did he fade away after the great Santa Claus debacle? Or is he still there in the dark of night, clearing out the monsters and creepy things along the path between your bed and the bathroom?

Some people have great confidence in the protection of angels, while others consign them to the "wouldn't that be nice?" category. And yet the Bible tells us that angels play a very active role in our lives, guarding us in *all* our ways. They even pick us up with their hands when we're in danger of stubbing our toes on a tiny little stone we never see. If a simple walk around the block requires angelic assistance, imagine how much work must go into a whole life!

Of course we have to remember not to make idols of the angels, who are only obeying the commands of God concerning us. Still, it's nice to have them around.

Father, thank You for the protection of the angels You have assigned
to my care. I may never be conscious of them in my life, but I know
they are there, doing Your will for my benefit.

Don't Be Led Astray

Little children,
let no man deceive you.
1 JOHN 3:7 KJV

It's easy enough to go astray with no help at all. At least then we only have ourselves to blame. But it gets more complicated when others are involved. Is your roommate to blame when the two of you go out for a night on the town and you overdo it? Did he lead you astray, or did you follow along with no encouragement at all?

There are plenty of people out there willing and able to lead you off in the wrong direction. Indeed, finding someone who wants to lead you in the right direction is pretty hard. But who is truly responsible when you fall? Certainly not God, and probably no other human being. The verse above says do not *let* anyone lead you astray. There's a choice involved, and it's up to you to make the final decision.

Father, give me the courage not to be a blind follower of others. Instead, help me see where others are heading, so I can get off the wrong path in time and follow Your way.

THE WHOLE PERSON

Charm is deceptive,
and beauty is fleeting;
but a woman who fears the Lord
is to be praised.
PROVERBS 31:30

This verse applies equally to men and women and should always be kept in mind during the dating years. Sure, everyone wants to date charming, beautiful people. Even those who are less than charming or beautiful themselves hope to connect with someone who qualifies.

But you can't choose a spouse on the basis of charm and looks alone. Neither can you rule out others on the basis of a lack of charm and beauty. Take a long, hard look in the mirror and then picture what you will look like in ten or twenty years. Don't you still hope to find someone to love the real you? Can you expect this from others and not give it to them in return?

Charm and beauty are simply attractants. Their job is to get someone's attention and give you the chance to win them. They're like the beautiful flower that makes it possible for a plant to reproduce, then fades away. It's the whole plant that's important, not just the flower.

Father, teach me to look beyond the surface and fall in love with a whole person, not just a pretty face.

Do You Want to Be a Slave?

The borrower is servant to the lender.
PROVERBS 22:7 KJV

It takes twelve years' work to graduate from high school or sixteen to get through college. That's years of books and papers, thousands of dollars invested in clothing, transportation, housing, and tuition. A diploma represents untaken vacations, overtime work, rent payments, and meals of hot dogs and beans instead of steak.

Did everyone go through all this so you could end up as someone's servant? But that's exactly what you will be if you grab your first credit card and pile on the fun. Who gets the first crack at your paycheck? The credit card people. They have to be paid first, month after month. It's a job you can't leave behind you—a servant's job. If your credit bill is high enough, you won't even be able to tithe, let alone save.

One credit card may be necessary for emergency use, but more than one only leads to disaster at this point in your life. You're a graduate, not a slave, so take control of your own life by taking control of your expenses.

Father, teach me how to live on what I make, not on my credit card limit. I don't need to be a servant to anyone but You.

GET A JOB

*For we hear that there are some which
walk among you disorderly,
working not at all, but are busybodies.
Now them that are such
we command and exhort by our Lord Jesus Christ,
that with quietness they work,
and eat their own bread.*

2 THESSALONIANS 3:11–12 KJV

Some people get away without working. A lot of them are young, still living at home, and being supported by their parents until they "find themselves." Well, what they need to find is a job. *Any* job.

There will always be those who are legitimately unable to support themselves, but we're not talking about them. We're talking about those who can't earn what they think they "deserve," those who are above taking a minimum-wage job and working their way up a rung at a time. Others can't find a "fulfilling" job. Ask your grandparents if their jobs were fulfilling and give them a good laugh. Sometimes just putting bread on the table is fulfillment enough.

God gave most of us the basic equipment necessary to earn a living: two hands, a strong back, and a nimble brain. You're not going to start at the top, but until you start somewhere, you're going nowhere.

*Father, thank You for giving me the ability to provide for myself.
The rest is up to me now.*

CHOOSING FRIENDS WITH CARE

A righteous man is cautious in friendship.
PROVERBS 12:26

We need friends at all stages of our lives, but especially when we're young and still trying to figure life out. Friends give us other viewpoints to consider. When we share experiences, we can save ourselves a great deal of time by avoiding some of our friends mistakes. We trust friends, often more than we trust our parents, because we have more in common with them.

Which is exactly why we need to be cautious in choosing our friends. Sometimes they betray us. Sometimes we discover they're not going in the direction we want to go, and it's hard to break up a friendship when we make this discovery.

Friendships also change as they mature, and sometimes these changes will hurt. Friends grow apart and then reconnect as time goes by, in a sort of cyclical flow—acquaintance, friend, acquaintance, friend again. A good friendship can tolerate these changes and grow stronger with each fluctuation. Choose your friends cautiously, and when you find a good one, hang onto him or her throughout your life.

Father, help me choose my friends with care and treasure those who stick by me through all life's ups and downs.

A REAL CHRISTIAN

"And they will seek my face;
in their misery they will earnestly seek me."
HOSEA 5:15

Leanne felt awful when she thought about the troubles her friend Maya had. She'd become a radiant Christian in college, but not long after, she had slid into unhappiness. Married a year after graduation, Maya was separated from her husband within months. From there, she got and lost jobs and never seemed to settle into adult life.

Maya had been a Christian; of that Leanne was sure. What had happened to her friend?

Not until they got together for lunch one day did Leanne begin to discover the truth. Maya did know Christ, but she hadn't given her whole life up to Him. A few major areas were "off limits" to God.

"God's been dealing with me through all this. He's been cleaning out the closets and making me a *real* Christian. I just had to hurt enough to come back to Him."

God doesn't want to make a Christian miserable, but He'll do what He has to do to get our attention. After all, He loves His children so much, He wants each by His side.

Thank You, Father, for loving me enough to let nothing keep us apart.

THE REASON GOD SAVES

Nevertheless he saved them for his name's sake,
that he might make his mighty power to be known.
PSALM 106:8 KJV

On their trip out of Egypt, the Israelites forgot God's miracles. They weren't even to the Promised Land, and already they were suffering from short-term memory loss!

Most of us could have understood if God had simply left this pigheaded people in the desert. "Find your own way!" each of us might have responded. "See if I care if you ever get out."

God isn't like that. When we disobey, He doesn't totally give up on us. But neither is His some wimpy compassion. He doesn't save us from our troubles just because, like a parent with a fussy child, He's tired of hearing our complaints.

The Lord of creation saves us to show the world what kind of stuff He's made of. How would anyone know what kind of God He is if He ignored our plight or constantly gave in to our whining? How would they know of His omnipotence?

He saves us because He's wonderful, not because we are.

Lord, thank You for loving me, even when I forget You. What a huge, glorious God You are!

GOD'S POWERFUL SWORD

For the word of God is living and active.
Sharper than any double-edged sword,
it penetrates even to dividing soul
and spirit, joints and marrow;
it judges the thoughts and attitudes of the heart.

HEBREWS 4:12

Have you ever picked up your devotional, read the Scripture, and felt as if God had written that verse especially for you? It went right to your heart because you were living out that verse.

The Bible isn't like any other book. Though you might enjoy a novel or learn a lot from a how-to book, neither reaches deep inside your soul the way Scripture does. The Word of God gets straight inside you and cuts to the truth in an instant. The Spirit can wield it like a sword, cutting sin out of your life.

But you have to hold still while God uses that sword; otherwise you can get all cut up. You'll leave a painful quiet time without the benefit of having the cancer of sin removed. Let God have His way with you, and though the sword might hurt at first, healing can come rapidly.

By the end of your prayers, you might feel whole again.

Holy Spirit, reach into my life with Your Word. Search out the places where sin hides and remove it from my life.

ELIJAH'S REST

Elijah was afraid and ran for his life.
1 KINGS 19:3

In a showdown with the priests of Baal, Elijah flourished God's power in their faces, while they couldn't even seem to get their deity's attention. It was a great spiritual victory.

Just when Elijah was on top of the world, wicked Queen Jezebel threatened to kill him. Terrified, Elijah ran.

Why would anyone who had seen God's power fear this woman? Wasn't Elijah wrong to run? Curiously, Scripture doesn't say that. Instead, God merely sent an encouraging angel to give Elijah rest.

One great spiritual victory didn't make the prophet cocky. Elijah didn't assume that because God had used him to outdo the priests of Baal not even the queen could touch him. He didn't feel invincible, he felt tired. Elijah needed a rest, not another battle.

When God has done great things in your life, do you leap ahead into new battles without being certain this is where God wants you to be? Be as obedient as Elijah and seek Him first.

Lord, I want to do great things for You, but more than that I want to be in Your will. Give me wisdom about which battles I need to take on.

A LOOK AT OUR NATION

Oh that thou wouldest. . .come down. . .
to make thy name known to thine adversaries,
that the nations may tremble at thy presence!
ISAIAH 64:1–2 KJV

When another nation takes a stand that, to us, is obviously against God's will, anger stirs our hearts. Like Isaiah, we may wish God would set the record straight in an act that would get the world's attention.

But before we ask God to wipe someone else out, we need to look at our own nation. No country made up of imperfect human beings will always do right. Thank God that mercy tempers His justice. Without that, we, too, would be wiped out.

God doesn't want us to ignore or excuse every wrong that happens in the world, but He doesn't want us just pointing the finger. Instead of setting ourselves up as critics, we need to reach out to individuals in need.

We can do that by encouraging our country to take right stands—whether it's at home or abroad. That way our nation can have a character pleasing to God.

Lord, I want to spread Your love to the world, but I need to start in my own neighborhood. Today, show me someone I can help.

HEARKEN TO GOD'S VOICE

"Today, if you hear his voice,
do not harden your hearts as you did . . .
during the time of testing in the desert."
HEBREWS 3:7–8

I guess my spiritual walk is as good as anyone's," Tim said. "I mean, I don't think I have to live like a pastor or anything, but I know God saved me."

"What do you mean?" Karl asked.

"Well, I can still enjoy myself, you know. All those rules in the Bible are really just for pastors."

Karl had never known that Tim's commitment level was so low. A serious Christian walk isn't something just for "professional Christians"—church leaders who get paid for their work. God calls every Christian to listen to Him every day.

Close your ears to Him, and like Tim, your heart starts to harden. Before long, you don't even realize how far you've strayed.

Open your heart to Him, and the gentle rains of the Spirit turn your life into a verdant garden.

Lord, I don't want to spend a lifetime in the desert when I can live in a garden. Show me today how I can do Your will.

BE FREE FROM THE OLD LIFE

For we know that our old self
was crucified with him . . .
that we should no longer be slaves to sin.
ROMANS 6:6

Giving up that old pair of sneakers is hard. Though you buy a new pair, for a while the old favorites hang around in the back of your closet and get used when you need to feel comfy.

Being a brand-new Christian can feel like those sneakers. The life before Christ still feels more comfortable. In those B.C. days, life wasn't so challenging. Snug in sin, you didn't change much. God wasn't pulling at your heart.

Let sin stay at the back of your closet, though, and you're denying the work God has already done in you. He says you're no longer a slave to sin. You don't *have* to give in when you feel it lurking.

Keeping the old temptations in your living space means sin will still creep in. Give in to sin, and except for the ache in your heart, you'll feel as if Jesus never saved you at all. Why be a slave, when God set you free?

Lord, cleanse me from my old life and fill me with Your sparkling new one.

CHRISTIANITY IN YOUR EVERYDAY LIFE

May the peoples praise you, O God. . . .
Then the land will yield its harvest,
and God, our God, will bless us.
PSALM 67:5–6

What does praise have to do with a good harvest? Unlike the Israelites, you may not go out to a field every day to earn your living. But that doesn't mean these verses don't apply to you. The principle that as a nation our physical blessings can never exceed our spiritual blessings still works.

Worship for God shouldn't be a separate cubbyhole, completely apart from our work lives. Our spiritual attitudes spill over into the things we do every day. When we have great relationships with God, we do better at our jobs, deal better with our coworkers, and truly aid people.

The nation that worships God and tells others of His wonders will be blessed. Suddenly the country's economy takes a turn for the better because people are being honest with one another. Those who once fought come to agreement.

All because its inhabitants recognized their Creator.

Lord, I praise You for the blessing You've poured out on my country.
May we turn to You in praise every day.

GENEROUS GIVING

"Give, and it shall be given unto you;
good measure, pressed down,
and shaken together, and running over,
shall men give into your bosom."
LUKE 6:38 KJV

You want me to what? Jake didn't say it, but he might as well have. His Sunday school teacher could see the thought on his face. As they continued discussing tithing, Jake didn't say much—his body language spoke for him. He crossed his arms and waited.

Finally Jake said, *"Ten percent?* I already give to God when I can afford it, and I do lots of things for the church. Isn't that enough?"

Stinginess with God really doesn't hurt Him. He already owns all creation. We only hurt ourselves when we try to bargain God down to 9 percent, 8 percent. . .and then point out our own good points to make up for our lack of giving.

God wants to give to a generous giver. But He can't give to you if you hold your cash tightly to your chest. How can you take when your hands are full?

Are your hands wide open today?

Lord, help me to understand Your blessing of giving. I want to be generous and open-hearted to You.

OPEN HEAVEN'S DOOR

He who has the Son has life;
he who does not have
the Son of God does not have life.
1 JOHN 5:12

Many non-Christians would like to believe that religion is a smorgasbord affair: You can take a little here, a little there, and come up with your own brand. Take what you like, and leave the rest behind! All enter heaven, no matter their beliefs.

Such people have often belittled Christians for their "narrow" idea that there is only one truth—only those who believe in Jesus enter heaven. Even if you're a firm believer, you may feel uncomfortable defining a truth that leaves so many outside heaven's gates. But you aren't being ruled by your own thinking or a nasty desire to exclude anyone. If that *were* true, you'd keep the Good News to yourself.

Sure it's easier to keep your mouth shut. But then wouldn't you be trying to exclude others? It would be like holding the door to heaven shut.

Are you opening heaven's door today?

Jesus, I know it's not popular to tell others that You are the only way to heaven. Don't let that stop me from telling them the truth.

A Noble Character

Who can find a virtuous woman?
for her price is far above rubies.
PROVERBS 31:10 KJV

When you date someone, do you look for the best-looking girl around, the guy with the most money—or a person with good character?

Dreams of your future spouse probably include a great-looking person, romantic evenings together, and wonderful conversations. You may not imagine a man who's truthful or a woman who treats her parents with respect.

God doesn't say you can't marry a good-looking mate or even one with a hefty bank account. But you could live without them. You can't live happily with a weak character.

Character doesn't look glamorous. You can't show off by sending your friend a picture of it. But you can live with it for a happy lifetime. You'll never worry where your mate is when you know he's trustworthy. You'll never fear a family get-together when you know she'll treat your parents kindly.

Is your date a noble character—or just a character?

Lord, character may not be the asset I'm dreaming of, but I know it's important. Turn my heart toward someone with a strong love for You and the willingness to do right.

THE WATER OF GOD'S SPIRIT

We instructed you how to live in order to
please God, as in fact you are living.
Now we ask you and urge you
in the Lord Jesus to do this more and more.
1 THESSALONIANS 4:1

Alice had known Jesus for years, but her spiritual life didn't have the zip her best friend Darla's had.

"I'm afraid to witness to anyone," Alice admitted. "I might bore them to death. What do you have that I missed out on?"

Sometimes being a Christian can turn into drudgery. We know the truth; we're not committing any "major" sins; but our spiritual life seems to have stagnated. Where did we go wrong?

When knowing God has as much excitement as a drive through a desert, check to see you're following the instructions He already gave you. Are you spending time with Jesus through regular Bible reading and prayer? Have you confessed *all* sin? Are you spending time with Christians who uplift you?

Like Alice, all Christians have dry spells. Just don't let your life become a desert. Search for the water of God's Spirit and drink deeply at His well.

Jesus, I don't want to live in a desert when I can drink of Your
Spirit. Fill me with Your love.

A Prophet in His Hometown

"Only in his hometown,
among his relatives and in his own house
is a prophet without honor."
MARK 6:4

If you're the first in your family to know *Jesus*, instead of just religion, you may have days when you get in heated discussions, hear all kinds of accusations, and almost wish you'd never been the one God called.

Breaking new ground for Jesus is tough. Everyone—even non-Christians—holds his or her spiritual beliefs firmly and with strong emotion. Sometimes Satan has a strong hold on people, and they struggle when they hear the truth.

When your siblings aren't polite about their thoughts on your faith, your parents ignore your witness, or your cousin says, "It's just a stage you're going through," stand firm. Even Jesus didn't get *everyone* to listen to Him, and the Old Testament prophets got more abuse than you probably ever will.

The witness still goes on, and people come to Jesus every day. Maybe soon it will be that cousin who belittled you.

Lord, I need to trust in You, even when people don't listen to my words. Keep me firm in faith, and give me the words You'd have me share with them.

A Clean Heart

And he said, "That which cometh out of the man,
that defileth the man.
For from within, out of the heart of men,
proceed evil thoughts."
MARK 7:20–21 KJV

"The devil tempted me, and I fell!" is no excuse for Christians. We can't get away with that line, any more than Adam got away with blaming Eve.

Though Satan is real and does tempt us, we can't evade our own responsibility. Jesus makes it clear that the real fault isn't in our environment, Satan, or anyone else. Our own sick hearts lead us into sin.

Jesus lived in the same pressure-cooker world we do, with sin all around Him, but He never gave in. Though religious leaders of His day erred, the Son of God stood firm in righteousness because His clean heart held no place for sin.

Left to ourselves, our case is hopeless—we can never change—but the Master is in the heart-cleaning business. Give Him yours today.

Lord, even when I want to be clean, my heart betrays me. Wash it clean in Your blood today.

Hope in the Midst of Despair

I have not a cake, but an handful of meal in a barrel,
and a little oil in a cruse:
and, behold, I am gathering two sticks,
that I may go in and dress it for me and my son,
that we may eat it, and die.
1 Kings 17:12 KJV

The widow of Zarephath was desperate. In the middle of a drought, she had no food and no hope of getting any. She gave up. It was the end for both her and her son.

In that moment, Elijah entered her life, and a seemingly chance meeting set her back on track. She didn't have roast beef every day, just enough food for her and her family, but God took care of her.

Like the widow, despair knows your name. But no matter what the situation, it isn't time to give up! Even when life seems impossible, God still has hold of the possibilities. Some days, you may lose hope. It seems as if God has forgotten you and the world is against you. But none of those thoughts come from God. He's told you He'll never fail you.

Help could be right around the corner!

Though I can't see the future, I know You can, Lord. Give me hope on those despair-filled days.

YOUR INVOLVEMENT IN POLITICS

Blessed be the Lord God of our fathers,
which hath put such a thing as this in the king's heart,
to beautify the house of the Lord which is in Jerusalem.
EZRA 7:27 KJV

Sometimes government seems out of control. You vote because you've learned that good citizens do that, but you wonder if you have any impact. As elected officials take part in evil acts, you wonder, *Is it worth it?* But if everyone who knows God steps out of the political process, wickedness only increases.

God may call you to help with the campaign of a politician with strong morality. Or you could write letters to congressional members, telling them how they should vote on an issue.

Do something else every day, too—pray. God changes the course of politics. He did that for Ezra, when King Artaxerxes, a pagan king, opened the door so that Ezra could help rebuild Jerusalem.

He can rebuild our nation, too.

When politics seems out of control, Lord, help me to remember that everything in life is under Your control.

A PIG IS A PIG

*Like a gold ring in a pig's snout is
a beautiful woman who shows no discretion.*
PROVERBS 11:22

Remember, the Jewish people have never held the pig in very high esteem. They would not think of wasting valuable gold to adorn an animal they believed unclean. After all, all the gold in the world would never make a pig clean. You might as well throw the gold into the ocean.

In the same way, beauty is wasted on an immoral woman. She may look good with her golden adornments and beautiful face, but a pig is a pig is a pig.

Does this sound harsh and unforgiving? Can't people change and reform? Of course they can. Unlike a pig, a person can be cleansed of sins through confession, forgiveness, and reformation. We all sin in various ways, and it's not for us to judge too harshly or refuse to recognize real change in a person.

But it is our job to use discretion in choosing our companions. Know who you are dating, keep your standards high, and don't be fooled by outward appearances.

Father, help me maintain my standards while avoiding judgment on the worth of others. It's a hard line to walk, but I know You will help me.

THE POT AND THE POTTER

"Woe to him who quarrels with his Maker."
ISAIAH 45:9

It's a good thing this verse doesn't say, "Woe to him who complains to his Maker," or we'd all be in trouble. As it is, we often skate on pretty thin ice, because quarreling, complaining, and moaning and groaning are all a little too close for comfort.

Why doesn't God "fix" the things that are wrong in our lives?

The Bible tells us we're just the clay He works with, and how often does a pot complain to the potter? "I'd like to be a little thinner, if you don't mind." It's a stupid idea, because the potter makes what he needs, and the clay has no voice in the creation. What does the clay know about the potter's needs and plans?

In the end, we and everything else in the world are whatever God wants us to be, and arguing about it is a waste of time and energy. Be the best pot you can be, and leave the rest to the Potter.

Father, I trust Your plans for me and my world. I don't know enough to argue about it, and it's not my place to do so. Forgive me when I become impatient.

THE WORLD'S MOLD

And be not conformed to this world:
but be ye transformed by
the renewing of your mind.
ROMANS 12:2 KJV

The world is full of amateur tailors trying to make us fit into their patterns, even if they have to squeeze and push us into them. If we don't fit, they will claim it's not because their pattern is wrong—something's wrong with us.

Some friends think a weekend without getting drunk is a waste of time. If they can't convince you to come along, they'll find someone else to spend time with, because you obviously don't fit in.

If you've got your mind straight, this won't bother you. You wouldn't wear a pair of jeans that came up to your knees, so why should you try to be something you aren't? You're not stamped out of a mold—you're an individual with your own mind. Don't let anyone convince you that you need to conform to their pattern.

Father, thank You for helping me set my own priorities. Give me the strength to resist those who want me to ignore my values and adopt their own.

Constant Love

For I am persuaded, that neither death, nor life,
nor angels, nor principalities, nor powers,
nor things present, nor things to come,
Nor height, nor depth, nor any other creature,
shall be able to separate us from the love of God,
which is in Christ Jesus our Lord.
ROMANS 8:38–39 KJV

A lot of things try to separate us from God. We trip on our own sins or over the feet of those we're walking with. We get "too busy" to attend church or too "educated" to trust the Bible. We often forget about God's love in our daily lives, turning to it only when we find ourselves in trouble. Our memory is pretty short, and God seems far away.

Yet none of this or "anything else in all creation" makes God give up on us. His love is always there for us, in good times or bad, success or failure, sin or sanctity. We can always go home to Him, no matter how far we stray.

You may have given up on yourself, but God hasn't. Accept His constant love and forgiveness, no matter how undeserving you feel.

Father, I often feel unworthy of anyone's love, especially Yours. In times like that, remind me that You will never give up on me.

GETTING PAST MISTAKES

Remember ye not the former things,
neither consider the things of old.
ISAIAH 43:18 KJV

The study of history is always profitable, as long as we don't get stuck in the past. "We've always done it this way" does not guarantee that we've always done it right. We need to respect the wisdom of experience without making a little god of it.

Dwelling on the past can stop you dead in your tracks. Suppose you went into a big meeting and made a total fool of yourself. Does that mean you should avoid all future meetings? Not if you learned from the experience and don't make the same mistake at every meeting. If you don't go to the meetings, you don't get ahead, so take the chance. Don't dwell on the past.

Life's full of embarrassing moments we'd prefer to forget, and people will usually allow us to put these moments behind us. After all, they have had their own share of such moments, and some of them have been bigger bloopers than any of yours.

Father, help me get past my mistakes and get on with my future, knowing You will help me guard my mouth and cover my back when needed.

VENGEANCE BELONGS TO GOD. . .ALONE

Rejoice not when thine enemy falleth, and
let not thine heart be glad when he stumbleth:
Lest the Lord see it, and it displease him,
and he turn away his wrath from him.
PROVERBS 24:17–18 KJV

Here's an interesting angle on why we shouldn't clap when our enemies suffer. Our natural tendency is to be happy when the bully finally hits the playground dirt or the dictator disappears some dark night. He's gotten away with it for too long, and we rejoice when he gets his due.

But God knows the bully and the dictator. One day His wrath will fall on them, without any help from us. He also doesn't want any cheering from the sidelines, any self-righteous gloating, any songs of joy—even ones that are hidden in our hearts. If He hears them, He will disapprove of them and turn away His wrath before the job is done. God respects everyone, good or bad, and expects us to do the same. We may not always be able to love our enemies the way God commands, but we don't have to show joy at anyone's downfall.

Father, sometimes it's hard to respect those who don't respect me, but justice is Your job, not ours. Teach me how to love my enemies as You command.

GENTLENESS

Let your gentleness be evident to all.
PHILIPPIANS 4:5

Gentleness doesn't seem to have much going for it today. It's macho time, every man for himself, and heaven help the weak. At least that's what the movies and television tell us, and a lot of people seem to be buying into it.

But movies and television aren't into reporting the truth. They're into entertaining, and gentleness can look boring, even in 3-D. For every graphic murder scene in the news, there are at least one thousand acts of kindness that go unreported. For every man who strikes out in anger, there are one thousand who reach out in peace. For every maniac oppressor, there are one thousand Peace Corps volunteers.

Once in awhile, you'll see a story about a good person—usually around Christmas—but John Wayne and Jimmy Stewart are dead. Who are our role models today? For the good of the world, "Let your gentleness be evident to all."

Father, teach me how to be that rare and endangered species—a gentle man, one who gives of himself for the benefit of others.

THE TEST OF YOUR FAITH

Examine yourselves, whether ye be in the faith;
prove your own selves.
2 CORINTHIANS 13:5 KJV

Oh, no, not another test! And it's not even going to be multiple choice.

Still, a little introspection is always a good idea. At least you'll know how far off the mark you've wandered. So what are the criteria here? Who gets an A and who fails?

First of all, this is an open-book test. Take your Bible and read all of Matthew. Read every word Jesus spoke and every command He ever gave. Point by point, how did you come out? Give yourself a grade on every command.

It could be kind of dismal until you hit Matthew 22: 37–39 (NIV): " 'Love the Lord your God with all your heart and with all your soul and with all your mind.' This is the first and greatest commandment. And the second is like it: 'Love your neighbor as yourself.' "

Now throw away your entire test. This is the only question that counts. By the way, the person doing the grading is you, and you can grade on a curve. Not so hard, was it?

Father, in a real test, I'm sure I'd fail, but You forgive me and only require my love. I can do that.

WORKING FOR THE LORD

Whatever you do, work at it with all your heart,
as working for the Lord, not for men,
since you know that you will receive
an inheritance from the Lord as a reward.
It is the Lord Christ you are serving.
COLOSSIANS 3:23–24

Are you miserable in your job? Mentally switch employers—imagine you work for God, not your boss.

Once you decide to work as if God were your boss, everything changes. You can't call in sick every Monday when God knows every healthy cell in your body. You can't give less than your best to God, who knows exactly how capable you are and wants to reward your efforts. If it takes fifty hours a week to get the job done, would you complain to God?

A few months of this, and your human supervisor is going to notice the change. You're getting the job done without resentment. Maybe you can be trusted, even promoted. She won't have the vaguest idea of what's come over you, but she'll be pleased, and supervisors who are pleased often turn into decent people. Try it.

Father, help me do all my work as if I were working for you, no matter how bad conditions are for me.

GOD'S FAITHFULNESS ABOUNDS

For what if some did not believe?
shall their unbelief make the faith of
God without effect?
ROMANS 3:3 KJV

We humans have a unique way of looking at the world: If we can't see it, it doesn't exist. Some really had a hard time believing the earth was round until they saw that little blue marble in pictures sent down from space. Others have no idea of how *big* a moose is until one is standing in the middle of the road, towering over their puny car. On television, they look a lot smaller.

But the earth has always been round, and the moose has always been big. Whether we've believed that or not, it's always been true.

Some people do not have faith for the same reason. They've never seen anything that proved God's faithfulness, so it doesn't exist for them. Does their disbelief make God's faithfulness disappear? If you say a moose is a big cow, isn't it still a moose? Things are what they are, no matter what we don't believe, and God is, and always has been, faithful to those who follow Him.

Father, You are who You are, unchangeable and forever. I may not be able to prove this, but I know it's true.

SPIRITUAL SIDELINES

Let us lay aside. . .
sin which doth so easily beset us. . . .
Looking unto Jesus. . .
who for the joy that was set before him endured the cross.
HEBREWS 12:1–2 KJV

You were enjoying a sport, not even thinking about your body, but getting into the game, when suddenly you moved the wrong way or someone hit you and down you went. In a flash, you moved from pleasure to pain. The doctor diagnosed a sprained ankle—and you couldn't play sports for a while.

Temptation sidelines you just like a sports injury. You're going along, minding your own business, and suddenly it hits. In one moment a new spiritual weakness entangles you. Cleaning out that sin may not happen overnight. You may have to turn to God many days—and many times in a day—until it no longer tempts you.

But don't give up when sin attacks. Just like that sports injury, if you do the right things, it will heal. Bring it to Dr. Jesus, and someday that temptation won't even draw you.

Lord, keep me from sin. But when I do fall, help me not to avoid the cross You've set before me.

Planning Notebooks

Commit to the Lord whatever you do,
and your plans will succeed.
PROVERBS 16:3

Wendy, your life is planned out to the final minute," Anne said with a little envy. "No one else knows just what they're doing three weeks from today at two o'clock."

Wendy liked to organize her life. Her large planning notebook outlined her schedule for the next month—dental appointments, dates, even birthdays of distant cousins. She'd also set down her future. In the back of her book she'd even listed specific career goals and dates to achieve them.

A few short years later, Wendy discovered that her career wasn't on schedule. Nowhere *near* on schedule! Suddenly life seemed to be one big disappointment.

When she confided her "failure" to Anne, her best friend pointed out some facts. "You may not have the fastest-growing career in the world, but people appreciate everything you do for them. You're well paid for your work, and you like what you do. You've had lots of chances to tell people about Christ, too. What's your beef?"

That night, during her prayer time, Wendy knew her life was running according to plan. But the plan was God's, not hers.

Lord, show me Your purpose for my life. I want my plans to be Your plans.

IN GOD'S IMAGE

So God created man in his own image,
in the image of God he created him;
male and female he created them.
God blessed them.
GENESIS 1:27–28

Y*ou* were created in God's image. God made you in a special design and blessed you.

But that special creation and blessing aren't yours alone. He also created and blessed the person you'll marry. Are you ready to treat your spouse as a person God has blessed? Do you remember that in His eyes you're *both* important? Can you keep each other from sin and encourage each other in your faith?

When you marry someone you know is created in God's image and realize just what that means, you don't mistreat your spouse. Though you may disappoint each other sometimes, you remember that this God-created person is special—not perfect. Sin may mar God's creation, but it cannot change the value of His work.

A believing man and wife are blessed by God. Even the most challenging life situations can't change that promise.

Jesus, I want to treat my spouse like a treasure from You. Help me see when I'm ready for the blessing of marriage.

God's "Special Someone"

Buy the truth, and sell it not.
PROVERBS 23:23 KJV

I f you tell my mother what happened, we're through," Rod stated emphatically.

Katie gave in to Rod's wishes, even though she thought he was being foolish. It wasn't that Rod had done anything wrong—until he lied to his mother and told her that the black eye came from a fall while skiing. Only Katie knew he'd actually been attacked by a couple of campus rowdies.

The lie burned into Katie's soul, though it didn't bother Rod at all.

Later Katie told the story to a friend. "I guess I should have known then that he wasn't a Christian, and I should have stopped dating him. But he talked like a Christian and seemed sincere in his faith. I never knew he was lying to me, either—just like he's lied to his mother. Stupid lies about unimportant things. Its like a sickness with him."

Katie had learned the hard way that Rod was not the "someone special" God had in mind for her. She stood up for her faith, and in time God brought along that special man for her.

Lord, I want to date the person You have in mind for me. I need Your wisdom to make the right decision, though.

When the Blind Lead the Blind

He also told them this parable:
"Can a blind man lead a blind man?
Will they not both fall into a pit?"
LUKE 6:39

What a delightful description Jesus gave us in this parable. You can easily see this pair ending in a pit, because neither can see the road.

Sometimes we're no better than these foolish men. Without even thinking of it, we hang on to someone who's going in the wrong direction. By the time we realize we've been following others, not God, we're on the edge of a crater.

Want to know if you will end in a spiritual hole? Look at the people you follow. Are they filled with peace and serving God, or are they running their own show, constantly dissatisfied with life?

Since you'll end up much like the people you follow most, be sure the people you emulate are worth following. Do they do what the Bible says is right? Are they honest and loving?

In the end, make sure you're following the greatest leader —Jesus. His paths don't go into pits.

Lord, I want to be a leader who won't bring others into a pit. Guide me this day to walk in Your footsteps.

THE MAGI

There came wise men from the east to Jerusalem,
Saying, Where is he that is born King of the Jews?
for we have seen his star in the east,
and are come to worship him.
MATTHEW 2:1–2 KJV

Who are the magi? Tradition names them, numbers them, and describes their entourage, but the Bible's story is meager.

Suddenly, in the biblical account, the mysterious magi appear from the east, stop on Herod's doorstep, and ask for the king of the Jews. They don't explain where they came from. We don't know why only *they* saw the star. Or why others didn't come from the south and north—and even across the sea, from the west.

We can be certain these men didn't come from around the corner—or East Jerusalem. To get to their destination, they had to follow a star, not a road map. Weeks before the birth of the child, they were probably already on their way. Through the star, God called them. They put out a lot of effort for a God they barely knew.

Yet some of us have trouble driving around the corner to church!

Thank You, Jesus, that You called me to Yourself as You did the wise men. I want to be ready to travel the distance.

DOING LAPS

The Israelites ate manna forty years ...
until they reached the border of Canaan.
EXODUS 16:35

You might call it "doing laps." Just as a swimmer goes back and forth in the pool to build up strength, sometimes God keeps us in the same place, doing the same thing, for a long time.

The Israelites complained that they didn't have food, so God gave them manna ... today and tomorrow and the next day. Boy, were they sick of that white, waferlike stuff! Like the swimmer in the pool, they never got anything different.

In our spiritual walk, when we get stuck "doing laps," we need to take a look at ourselves. Maybe, like the Israelites, we've sinned, and God is trying to humble us. Or maybe we need to gain strength, so God has us exercising the same spiritual muscle over and over again.

If you're doing laps, search your heart. Do you need to confess some sin so you can move on? If not, don't get discouraged. God is building up your strength.

That's why you're diving into the water one more time.

Lord, when I feel waterlogged, show me why I'm diving into the water again.

MORAL CHOICES

As ye have always obeyed,
not as in my presence only,
but now much more in my absence,
work out your own salvation
with fear and trembling.
PHILIPPIANS 2:12 KJV

Now that you are on your own, it's easy to think, *Mom and Dad aren't here to yell at me. I'll just do things my way.* Well, when it comes to how you vacuum your apartment, it doesn't matter if you don't obey Mom and Dad's rules, as long as things get clean. But moral choices *do* matter.

Mom and Dad might not be there at midnight, when you have to decide whether or not to invite your date to your apartment for "a cup of coffee." But soon you'll find you won't just be doing the wrong thing on your date, you'll be lying about how you spent the weekend.

Whether or not Paul was there, the Philippians toed the line morally. Perhaps they understood that they weren't obeying Paul, but God. Paul wasn't being a rule maker. He showed them the best way to have a terrific relationship with God. They wanted that, so they followed the "rules."

Father God, sometimes Your ways seem so restrictive. I need to remember they're leading me to a happier, more holy life.

LISTEN TO YOUR FATHER

Now therefore hearken, O Israel,
unto the statutes and unto the judgments,
which I teach you, for to do them, that ye may
live, and go in and possess the land which the
Lord God of your fathers giveth you.
DEUTERONOMY 4:1 KJV

Do you avoid obeying God's Word and only approach Him when you need something?

If so, you probably struggle in your Christian walk. Seeing God as a sort of "celestial Santa Claus" shows a selfishness that separates you from God's blessing.

The nation of Israel followed God when it was convenient. They got a blessing—the Promised Land—but only on a forty-year revised schedule.

Obey God because you love Him and want to be more like Him, and He gives you your Promised Land immediately, not forty years late. His blessings are real, but not automatic.

God's giving isn't tit for tat—it's all-out sharing from a Father who loves children who listen to Him. But He can't reward disobedient children.

So listen to your Father.

Father, I know You want to bless me. Keep me from sin that ruins blessing.

GREETING THE OUTCAST

Thou shalt neither vex a stranger,
nor oppress him:
for ye were strangers in the land of Egypt.
EXODUS 22:21 KJV

You move to a new town or a new school, and for the first few days you feel really strange. You don't know where to go for anything you need. You don't know who to ask for advice.

Then someone comes along and tells you about some good stores, the best bank, and maybe a great doctor. All of a sudden you're beginning to find your feet. You feel more secure, and life balances out again.

God knows what it feels like to be in a strange place (After all, didn't Jesus leave His home to come to earth?). He understands that sometimes you have to go to a new place (Didn't he call Abram to move?).

Maybe because of that, He tells us to have compassion for the new person on the block. We don't need to wonder if we should stretch out a welcoming hand. God's been there before us, greeting the outcast.

Thank You, Lord, for caring for me when I'm in a new place. Help me to reach out to others who are feeling strange in a new town, a new job, or a new country.

THE SAVIOR'S LIGHT

For unto you is born this day
in the city of David a Savior,
which is Christ the Lord.
LUKE 2:11 KJV

What an unusual night that was for a ragged bunch of shepherds huddled out in the cold! After being nearly scared to death by an angel reflecting God's splendor, they heard the wonderful Good News that God had fulfilled His promise. Then they, of all people, were invited to witness what God had done.

The shepherds could hardly wait to go to Bethlehem. Imagine! Through the ages Hebrews had waited for this and, unworthy as they were, *their* eyes were about to see Messiah!

They hurried off, not to see a king in his might, but a peasant baby in a common stable—a person much like them. Respected religious leaders probably would have sneered at such an unlikely Redeemer. But the humble shepherds trusted in the One who God showed them that night, and His light filled their lives.

Are you overflowing with the Savior's light? Ask God to forgive your sins and let Him take charge of your life, and the true meaning of Christmas will flood your soul, too.

Jesus, I want Your light to fill every part of my being. During this special season, let me show others the light You bring.

THE LORD LOOKS AT THE HEART

"Man looks at the outward appearance,
but the Lord looks at the heart."
1 SAMUEL 16:7

J osh can't be a Christian!" Sheila exclaimed. "He may come to church, but he just sits in the pew. Have you ever known him to take part in anything but Sunday mornings or help out in any way? And look at those friends he brings to church —each one looks as if he'd be more at home at a bikers' convention than here!"

Too bad Sheila couldn't see into Josh's heart. Her judgments couldn't have been more wrong. In some areas Josh got a slow start as a Christian, but his warm heart for bikers led him to reach out to people the church rarely touched. A few years later, his ministry to these people bore much fruit.

Thank God that He sees beyond our brothers' and sisters' criticisms and into our hearts. Sin can't hide our real value or keep Him from lifting us out of its mire.

Are you plopped in mire today or reaching out to God?

Thank You, Lord, for seeing my heart, not just my actions. Make me clean from the inside out.

Inspirational Library

Beautiful purse/pocket-size editions of Christian classics bound in flexible leatherette. These books make thoughtful gifts for everyone on your list, including yourself!

When I'm on My Knees   The highly popular collection of devotional thoughts on prayer, especially for women.
    Flexible Leatherette.................$4.97

The Bible Promise Book   Over 1,000 promises from God's Word arranged by topic. What does God promise about matters like: Anger, Illness, Jealousy, Love, Money, Old Age, and Mercy? Find out in this book!
    Flexible Leatherette.................$3.97

Daily Wisdom for Women   A daily devotional for women seeking biblical wisdom to apply to their lives. Scripture taken from the New American Standard Version of the Bible.
    Flexible Leatherette.................$4.97

My Daily Prayer Journal   Each page is dated and features a Scripture verse and ample room for you to record your thoughts, prayers, and praises. One page for each day of the year.
    Flexible Leatherette.................$4.97

Available wherever books are sold.
Or order from:

Barbour Publishing, Inc.
P.O. Box 719
Uhrichsville, OH 44683
http://www.barbourbooks.com

If you order by mail, add $2.00 to your order for shipping.
Prices are subject to change without notice.